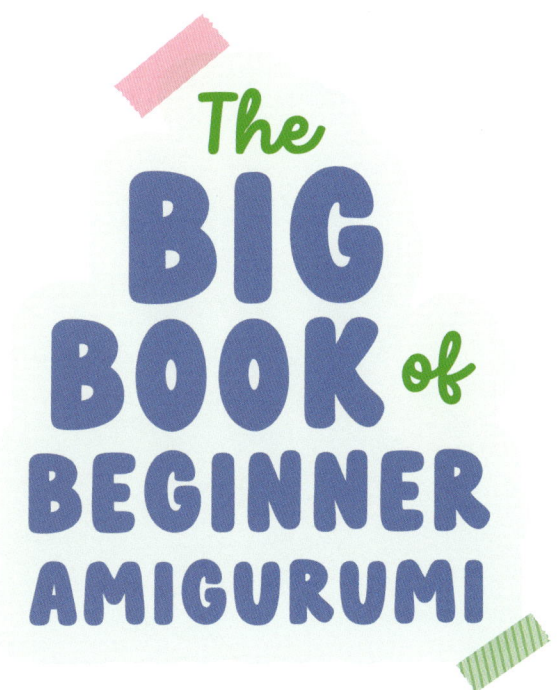

The **BIG BOOK** of **BEGINNER AMIGURUMI**

The
BIG
BOOK of
BEGINNER
AMIGURUMI

60 EASY PROJECTS FOR CHARMING CROCHET CREATIONS

Maggy & Pippa Woodley

PAGE
PAGE STREET
PUBLISHING CO.

PAGE STREET
PUBLISHING CO.

First published in 2026 by

Page Street Publishing Co.

27 Congress Street, Suite 1511

Salem, MA 01970

www.pagestreetpublishing.com

Distributed by Macmillan, sales in Canada by The Canadian Manda Group.

30 29 28 27 26   1 2 3 4 5

ISBN-13: 979-8-89003-466-3

Edited by Marissa Giambelluca

Cover and book design by Vienna Gambol for Page Street Publishing Co.

Photography by Maggy and Pippa Woodley

Printed and bound in China

TO GRANNY AND GRANDPA,
FOR ALWAYS BEING
OUR BIGGEST FANS AND
CONSTANTLY SUPPORTING US
ON OUR CREATIVE JOURNEYS.

TABLE of CONTENTS

Introduction

We are a mother and daughter team who love all things crafty, and we have been crafting and creating together for fifteen years.

A word from Maggy: As a young girl, I spent a lot of time with a wonderful woman called Celia, whom we called our adoptive Granny. Celia used to come and stay with us for a few days or weeks here and there, when my parents needed some help. She taught me how to sew, knit, and bake, and she always encouraged me to pursue my artistic endeavors and to learn more skills. The patience and creative love she shared with me, I now pour into my website: Red Ted Art. My passion has always been about encouraging people to "have a go": to learn skills new to them while always keeping the old skills in sight. Everyone should be able to sew a little and at least have had a go at knitting and crochet. As part of this "learn something new" ethos, I taught myself to crochet twelve years ago—especially since crochet lends itself to adorably cute projects (in my eyes, much more so than knitting!).

I am so excited that crochet has become what it is today. Goodbye to crochet doilies of old, and hello to the adorable world of amigurumi!

A word from Pippa: Having grown up in a household full of crafting and creativity, I was always eager to try new things. My crochet journey actually began with knitting! I learned to knit when I was around seven or eight years old. I was never actually that good at knitting because I found it difficult to cast on the stitches, and I would always make mistakes. I was also frustrated at the fact that all the knitting patterns seemed to be mostly pillows and blankets or items of clothing. There wasn't a cute plushie pattern in sight!

That's when my mother showed me the wonders of the crochet world—hundreds of different adorable amigurumi, irresistible to make. When COVID-19 struck and we all went into the first lockdown, this offered me the perfect opportunity to learn a new skill: crochet! My mother offered to teach me, so I decided to give it a go. It went terribly. I couldn't even make a slip knot. I was so frustrated by how confusing and difficult crochet seemed. So, I gave it a little break.

When we went into the next lockdown a few months later, I gave it another go. This time, I managed to make a granny square after hours of trying. Soon after that granny square, I was able to progress quickly and extend my skills to create adorable projects.

After persevering and learning a skill that I love, I started to create my own patterns to share my passion with other people and encourage them to step out of their comfort zone and try something new.

The moral of the story: Don't give up! Crochet is a wonderful skill to have, and once you get over the initial hurdles of being that brand-new beginner, you can learn and progress very quickly! In this book, we'll help you master the basics so you can create fun amigurumi to share with your family and friends.

Pippa & Maggy

To Sew or Not to Sew

This is a much-discussed topic in the crochet community! Many people are constantly on the hunt for the perfect "no-sew" crochet patterns, since they sound like they should be quick and easy to make. Some crocheters also seem to find sewing incredibly boring and "chore-like" when they are creating different pieces.

Is sewing really that bad? We certainly don't think so. Here are some things to consider:

1. "No-sew" projects often come with more complicated stitches (e.g., the bobble stitch), which aren't very beginner-friendly and can be frustrating to create.

2. Some "no-sew" projects require inserting your hook into sealed-off work to add parts such as ears or tails, which can be very finicky. On top of that, most of them are really "low-sew" projects (at best), because you will always need to embroider a cute mouth or nose, seal the hole of the magic circle, and weave away loose ends!

3. Sewing allows you more creative freedom when you are making different projects, ranging from incredibly simple ones to those that are complicated and intricate.

As part of being a successful crocheter, you'll find that basic skills such as sewing will enhance your crocheting ability to produce those amazing and cute results. Sewing also allows you to easily personalize and add features to your crochet creations without needing to worry about mastering complicated stitches or putting your crochet hook into awkward positions.

Overall, we firmly believe that you shouldn't see sewing as a boring chore. Instead, you can view it as a way to improve and add more cuteness to your finished pieces.

Tools and Materials

Here, we outline the supplies used throughout the book. However, the patterns are designed for you to make the most of what you have on hand. As a beginner, you don't need to buy expensive supplies. Check out the notes marked as Top Tips for more advice.

CROCHET HOOKS

For all of the patterns in this book, we used a US D/3 hook size (3.25mm). We recommend using a metal crochet hook, since many plastic hooks have rough edges that can get caught in your work or are very flimsy, making them breakable and difficult to hold.

With that in mind, to create these patterns, you can use any hook size of your choice as long as it matches the yarn you have. The recommended hook size for each type of yarn usually appears on the yarn packaging.

Top Tip: If you don't have the yarn packaging or it doesn't mention the hook size, you can determine which hook to use by comparing it to the thickness of the yarn. If the hook is roughly the same thickness as the yarn, then that's the one to use!

YARN

All the projects in this book were made and designed using acrylic DK/light worsted/3 ply yarn. Many brands make yarn like this. It is the most affordable yarn, too, and it is available in most craft stores.

That said, the patterns have been tested using various types of yarn, such as plush yarn or cotton, which are both popular with amigurumi projects. All the patterns in this book can be made using any yarn of your choice—just make sure that you use a corresponding hook size!

Top Tip: Using different yarns will result in different-sized projects! This is a fun way to make different-sized amigurumi and turn an amigurumi mini (e.g., for a key chain) into a plushie. With that in mind, many beginners find plush yarn challenging to work with because it is harder to see the stitches and it can get knotted. For super-plush yarn, you will also need extra-secure safety eyes that are suitable for the plushies or sew-on eyes that won't fall through the holes of the big stitches. For all of these reasons, we suggest that you move on to plushies only when you are confident making these patterns with DK yarn first.

EMBROIDERY NEEDLE

This is a chunky, blunt needle with a large eye big enough to fit your yarn through it. We will use this throughout the book when attaching parts and sealing up any holes or gaps in your crochet.

STUFFING

We used polyester toy stuffing for the crochet creations. This stuffing is available in all haberdasheries or craft stores. To help get the stuffing into tight spaces, you may want to use the back of a crochet hook to push it in.

Top Tip: To save on resources and simply get started, you can also use leftover yarn scraps for stuffing, or clean stuffing from a pillow that you have washed.

SCISSORS

You need a good pair of small and sharp scissors that can cut yarn effectively.

SAFETY EYES

Throughout the book, we used 6mm safety eyes for these projects. Depending on your preference and crochet size, you may want to use smaller or larger safety eyes on your work.

Note: If you are making something for a small child, safety eyes can be a choking hazard if they are not correctly put in. Consequently, safety eyes are not recommended to be used for children under three years of age. Create eyes on your project with embroidery for this age group instead.

STITCH MARKERS

When you are working in a circular shape, stitch markers come in handy. They help prevent you from losing track of where you are in the project.

Top Tip: If you do not have any stitch markers—or keep losing them like we do!—you can use a piece of yarn, a paper clip, or a safety pin.

PINS

You may wish to use some pins to secure any limbs that need sewing on to help keep things in place.

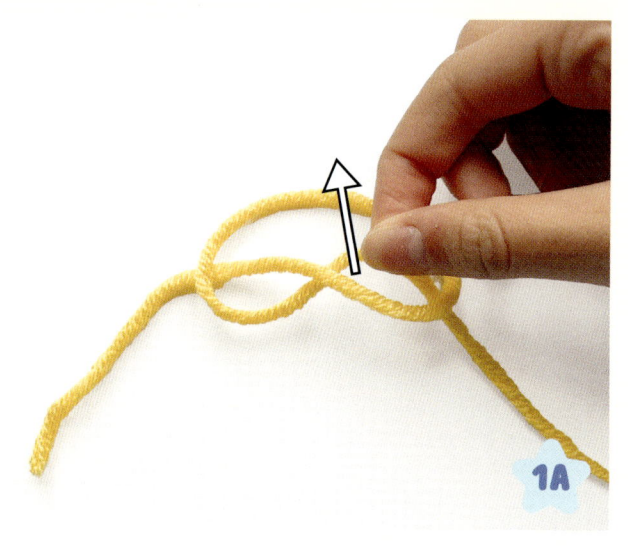

1A

1B

3A

3B

3C

4

Beginners' Techniques

In this section, we will be covering some basic—yet important—techniques that you will use for the patterns in the book. These techniques allow you to easily enter the world of crochet, helping you to build and improve your skills.

ABBREVIATIONS

The projects in this book use the most common crochet techniques, and U.S. crochet terminology is used throughout. This may seem like a long list of stitches, but once you get going, you will see that you are using the same basic abbreviations throughout. A handful of patterns use the half double crochet (hdc) and triple crochet (tc), simply to give you the opportunity to try these out and learn!

Rnd(s) – round(s)

Ch – chain

Sc – single crochet

Slst – slip stitch

Inc – single crochet increase

Dec – single crochet decrease

3tog – 3 stitches together

FLO – front loop only

BLO – back loop only

Hdc – half double crochet

Dc – double crochet

Tr – triple crochet

Mc – magic circle

Dc inc – double crochet increase

Dc dec – double crochet decrease

Hdc inc – half double crochet increase

A BRIEF OVERVIEW OF THE BASIC STITCHES

Making a Chain (Ch)

1. Begin by creating a slip knot.

2. Put your hook through the slip knot, and pull the ends of the yarn to tighten it. With the long piece of yarn, create your tension with your nondominant hand.

3. Yarn over and pull the yarn through the loop that is on your hook.

4. Repeat yarning over and pulling through the loop on your hook until you reach the number of chains that you require.

3A

3B

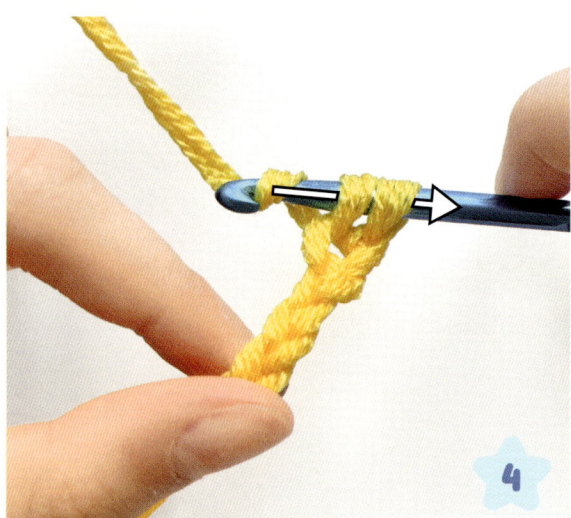

4

Single Crochet (Sc)

1. To create a single crochet, you need to have some form of a base to work into, so begin by creating a chain.

2. As you make a single crochet into a chain, always skip the first chain (the one that is closest to your hook). This is because it is very difficult to work into the first chain.

3. Push your hook through the top of the next chain, yarn over and pull through that loop. You should now have two loops on your hook.

4. Yarn over and pull through the two loops on your hook. This is your single crochet completed.

5. Repeat as many times as needed.

Slip Stitch (Slst)

The slip stitch is very similar to the single crochet stitch.

1. Begin by inserting your hook through the next stitch.

2. Yarn over and pull through that stitch. Then continue pulling that same piece of yarn through the loop on your hook.

3. This is your slip stitch.

Increase (Inc)

The technique used to create an increase stays the same for every type of stitch. To increase, you work two stitches into the same stitch.

1. Begin by creating a stitch.
2. Instead of moving on and going into the next stitch, go back into the same stitch that you just worked in, and then create another stitch. This should form two stitches in one stitch.

Decrease (Dec)

The technique used to create a decrease stays the same for every type of stitch. With this technique, you crochet two stitches together to create one stitch.

1. Start by inserting your hook into the next stitch. Yarn over and pull through.
2. Instead of yarning over again and pulling through the remaining loops, insert your hook into the next stitch.
3. Yarn over and pull through that stitch.
4. Yarn over again, and pull through all three loops on your hook. You have now crocheted two stitches together to create one stitch.

Note: The image shows a single crochet increase. Increases/decreases are done in the same way for all stitch types—whether single crochet, double crochet, or half double crochet!

3 Stitches Together (3tog)

This technique is essentially a decrease, (as shown in the image above) but instead of crocheting two stitches together to create one stitch, you are crocheting three stitches together to create one stitch.

1. Start off by inserting your hook into the next stitch. Yarn over and pull through.

2. Instead of yarning over again and pulling through the remaining loops, insert your hook into the next stitch.

3. Yarn over and pull through that stitch.

4. Insert your hook into the next stitch. Yarn over and pull through that stitch.

5. You should now have four loops on your hook. Yarn over and pull through all four loops.

6. Repeat as many times as needed.

Front Loop Only (FLO)

This only applies when you are working into stitches such as single crochets and double crochets—not chains. This is because single and double crochet stitches have a V-shaped top that is easy to work into.

1. Identify the V shape on your next stitch. One side of the V should be facing toward the back of your crochet, and the other side should be facing toward the front of your crochet.

2. Instead of inserting your hook through both the loops as usual, only insert your hook through the loop that is facing the front of your crochet (hence the name Front Loop Only).

3. Work your stitch as usual. Repeat as many times as needed.

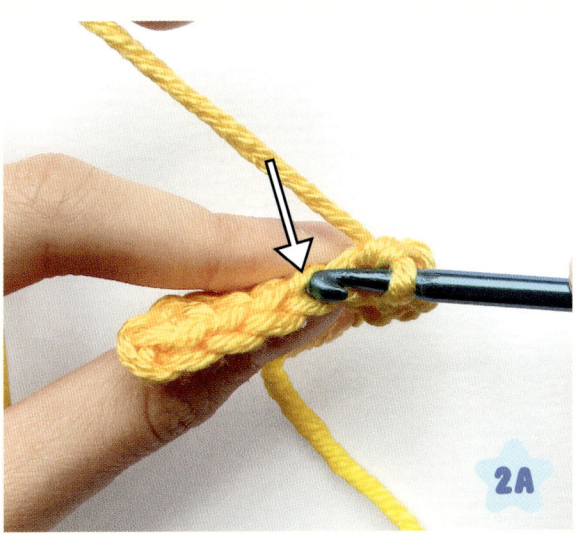

2A

2B

Back Loop Only (BLO)

This only applies when you are working into stitches such as single crochets and double crochets—not chains. This is because single and double crochet stitches have a V-shaped top that is easy to work into.

3

1. Identify the V shape on your next stitch. One side of the V should be facing toward the back of your crochet, and the other side should be facing toward the front of your crochet.

2. Instead of inserting your hook through both the loops as usual, only insert your hook through the loop that is facing the back of your crochet (hence the name Back Loop Only).

3. Work your stitch as usual. Repeat as many times as needed.

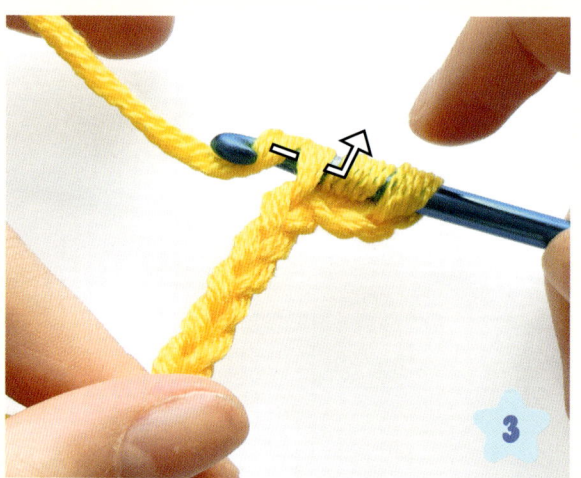

Half Double Crochet (Hdc)

1. Start by creating a chain so you have a base to work into. (If you're working in rounds, you will just use the next stitch.)

2. Yarn over (so you have the yarn wrapped around your hook once), and insert your hook into the next stitch.

3. Yarn over and pull through that stitch. You should now have three loops on your hook.

4. Yarn over and pull through all three loops on your hook. This is your half double crochet finished.

Double Crochet (Dc)

Note: The first three steps are the same as the half double crochet!

1. Start by creating a chain so you have a base to work into. (If you're working in rounds, you will just use the next stitch.)

2. Yarn over (so you have the yarn wrapped around your hook once), and insert your hook into the next stitch.

3. Yarn over and pull through that stitch only. You should now have three loops on your hook.

4. Yarn over and pull through the first two loops only on your hook. You should now have two loops remaining on your hook.

5. Yarn over and pull through the remaining two loops. This is your double crochet finished.

Triple Crochet (Tr)

1. Start by creating a chain so you have a base to work into. (If you're working in rounds, you will just use the next stitch.)

2. Yarn over twice, so you have the yarn wrapped around your hook twice. Insert your hook into the next stitch.

3. Yarn over and pull through that stitch only. You should now have four stitches on your hook.

4. Yarn over and pull through the first two stitches on your hook. You should now have three stitches left on your hook.

5. Yarn over and pull through the first two stitches again. You should now have two stitches left on the hook.

6. Finally, yarn over and pull through the last two stitches on your hook. This is your triple crochet completed.

Magic Circle (Mc)

The magic circle, or magic ring, is probably the most challenging part of crochet because it is very confusing to create at first—so don't feel disheartened if you're unable to create it on your first try!

1. Create a loop with your yarn. Yarn over and pull the yarn through the loop, but do not tighten the stitch—you want it to stay loose.

2. Hold the loop that you have created open, and make a chain.

3. Put your hook through the loop, and treat it like a stitch. Create a single crochet.

4. Go back into the same loop continuously until you have made the right number of stitches.

5. There should be a short yarn tail poking out the side of the ring. Pull it gently to tighten the ring. Sometimes if you pull it too hard, the yarn can snap or get stuck inside the stitches, so make sure to pull it gently.

![Crochet hook with yellow yarn forming stitches, labeled with a blue star numbered 4.]

Magic Circle Alternative

Top Tip: If you are struggling to get the hang of the magic circle, do not worry! You can use this easier alternative instead.

1. Make a chain of 2.

2. Into that second chain from the hook, create as many stitches as needed into the same loop. For example, if you need to make 6sc into a mc, you can just create 6 single crochets all into the second chain.

Although this may seem like an amazing alternative, it is less neat than the magic circle, and you will have a small hole in the middle that you will struggle to get rid of. Consequently, we recommend taking the time to master the magic circle once you are more comfortable with these techniques.

ADDING FACIAL FEATURES TO YOUR AMIGURUMI

Adding facial features is a very important part of amigurumi because it gives your finished amigurumi a cute and irresistible little face. Most of the patterns throughout the book have a sweet little smile or nose.

You can buy plastic noses and eyes to attach to your work (e.g., safety eyes), but we think the embroidery of these details looks much better and really gives your work a personal touch. Make sure that after finishing each facial feature, you fasten off your yarn by weaving it around your creation and then cutting off the leftover yarn.

Let's take a look at how to add your features.

How to Sew a Mouth

1. To create the mouth, sew a straight line between the two eyes.

2. Move the needle to the row underneath the straight line.

3. Move it into a position where it is directly in line with the middle of the stitch created.

4. Pull the yarn up and under the stitch. Then do a normal running stitch downward and back into the same stitch you came out of.

How to Sew on a Flat Beak

1. Sew a running stitch directly between the two eyes.

2. Sew another running stitch over the top of the last running stitch to make the beak thicker.

How to Sew a Pointy Beak

1. From the middle of the two eyes, sew a running stitch that goes down a round below the eyes.

2. Next to the last stitch made, sew two more stitches that also go down to make the beak thicker.

3. To make the beak neater and have a more triangular shape, sew a running stitch between the eyes that goes over the top of the three stitches made.

How to Sew on an Animal Nose (T-Shaped)

1. Sew a running stitch directly between the two eyes.

2. To make the top of the nose thicker, sew another running stitch over the top of the last running stitch.

3. Move the needle to the row underneath the straight line.

4. Move it into a position where it is directly in line with the middle of the stitches created.

5. Sew a running stitch upward, so it reaches the bottom of the nose.

2

3A

3B

3C

3D

3E

How to Sew on Hair

This is a beginner-friendly way to attach hair to your doll and make it look great!

1. Cut 30 pieces of yarn approximately 8 inches (20 cm) long.

2. Place the bundle of hair onto the head of your doll and position it however you would like. Just make sure it covers the whole head.

3. Cut a long piece of yarn that is the same color as the hair. (In the image we've used a different color just to make it easier for you to see our stitches.) Then use an embroidery needle to sew stitches down the center of the head, over the top of the hair, to hold the hair in place. As you do this, sew a stitch over every three to four strands of hair, to make it even.

This should sew the hair into place and give your doll a cute parting!

Don't worry if the back of your doll almost looks a bit bald. Just style the hair down and position it so there aren't any bald spots. You can also add some extra stitches to the back of the hair to keep it in place. You can also trim and style the hair further if you wish.

3

4A

USEFUL TECHNIQUES
How to Seal a Magic Circle

Once you get to the end of your project and it's time to fasten off, close the untidy hole to make sure your amigurumi looks the best it can be.

4B

1. Cut off your yarn and leave a long tail.

2. Attach an embroidery needle to the yarn, and weave the yarn through all the front loops of the remaining stitches.

3. Pull the yarn tail gently, so the hole closes. Sometimes if you pull it too hard, the yarn can snap or get stuck inside the stitches.

4. Weave the remaining yarn through your project (away from the hole), and cut it off. This final weaving step helps ensure that the hole won't reopen.

How to Crochet Two Sides/Edges Together

Sometimes you may need to crochet two sides together to create one flat edge. Here's how.

1. Line up the two sides that are going to be crocheted together, so the opposite stitches are in line with each other.

2. Put your hook through the next stitch, and then put it through the opposite stitch.

3. Create a single crochet (or whatever stitch you are using) as normal. Repeat as many times as needed.

The **BIG BOOK** of **BEGINNER AMIGURUMI**

How to Work on the Other Side of a Chain

This technique may seem quite confusing at first, but it is relatively simple once you get the hang of it. Working on the other side of a chain will give you an oval shape.

1. Create your chain and complete the stitches that are required in the pattern. Our example shows a single crochet.

2. Once you reach the end of the chain, instead of chaining 1 and turning to create the next round, continue on the opposite side of the chain you have just worked into, as follows.

3. Look at your piece, and identify how one side has a row of stitches, while the other side just has a row of loops.

4. To proceed, put your hook into the nearest loop to you. Create your stitch as normal.

5. Keep going into these remaining loops until you reach the end of the chain.

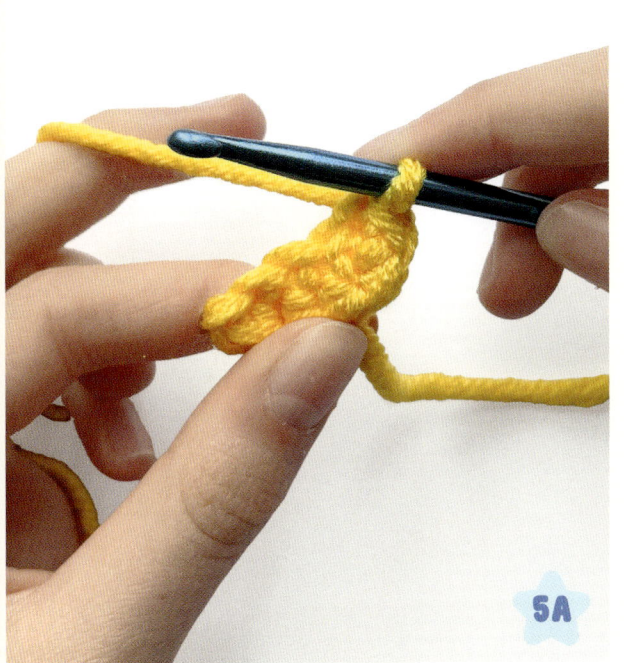

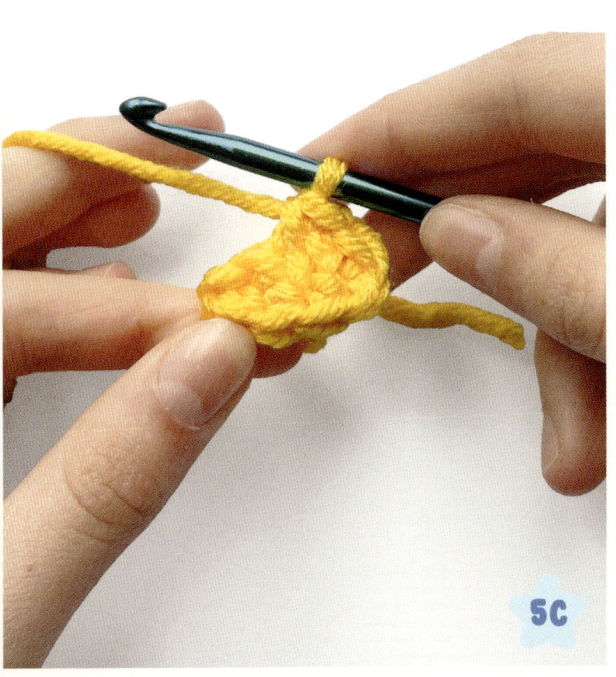

Joining Legs

In some of the patterns, you are required to make two separate legs and then join them to carry on with the body. Here's how.

1. Make sure that your hook is attached to your second leg. Insert your hook into the side of the first leg. (To be able to achieve this, you may need to create a chain before inserting the hook, depending on your pattern.)

2. Create your stitch as normal. Carry on crocheting in the first leg until you reach the end of the round.

3. Instead of carrying on in the first leg, insert your hook into the closest stitch of the second leg. Then complete your stitch. (If you made a chain previously, then you will have to work into the back of that chain first.)

3A

3B

3C

4A

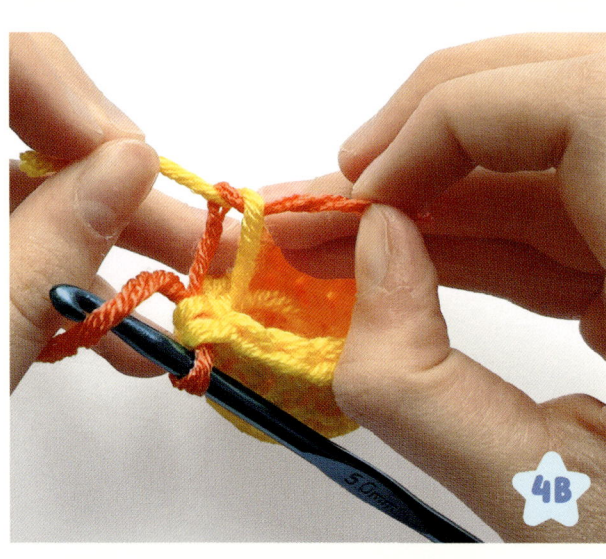

4B

5

Color Change

Changing color is an important part of crochet and amigurumi, as it allows your work to have different designs and patterns.

1. Start by inserting your hook into the next stitch. Yarn over and pull through.

2. Instead of yarning over again and pulling through the remaining loops, grab another color of yarn.

3. Fold that yarn in half, and hook the yarn with the crochet hook. Pull the yarn through the remaining two stitches on your hook.

4. Cut off the yarn of your original color. Tie the end of the yarn that you just cut to the tail end of the new yarn, and form a knot.

5. Carry on crocheting as usual.

Note: With this most common and easiest form of color change, you will always have a "lip" in your work. Designers create their patterns for these color changes to usually be on the side, back, or bottom of your work. The "lip" is normal—especially for beginners and intermediate crocheters—so don't fret if you see this in your work.

ASSEMBLING TIPS

1. Make sure that you leave a tail after cutting any yarn. This tail allows you to sew things into place or close any holes.

2. If you are struggling to get stuffing into your projects, you can use a chopstick or the back of your crochet hook to help poke the stuffing into those small spaces.

3. After sewing things into place, weave the leftover tail through the main body of your project a couple of times to prevent it from falling off. As you are doing this, always go back into the same stitch that you came out of to make sure you do not create any big stitches over the top of your work by accident.

4. Pin features into place before you sew them on so they don't move around as you are trying to sew.

5. If you are following the pattern exactly but you don't like the intended positioning, feel free to change it to suit you! Sometimes you don't have to follow the pattern exactly to get a cute outcome that you are happy with.

Kawaii FOOD

Food—glorious food! When it comes to amigurumi and kawaii crochet patterns, inanimate objects such as food are generally very popular . . . especially when you start adding adorable faces and maybe even some fun little feet!

The Kawaii Food section is not only super-cute, but it really is the easiest part of this book! These patterns will help you get warmed up and feel confident reading basic patterns, adding some faces, and learning how to sew on little details, such as a leaf or stem.

These projects will also allow you to practice some of the very basics of making amigurumi. After you learn to make a simple ball shape (e.g., the Apple on page 47), you can extend what you've learned to make other shapes (e.g., the oval Pineapple on page 55). Let's dive in!

APPLE

Let's begin with the apple—the round classic. Make this in green or red! It's perfect as a little back-to-school keychain or an end-of-the-year teacher's gift.

APPLE BODY

Starting at the top
In red

Rnd 1: 6sc into mc [6]

Rnd 2: 6inc [12]

Rnd 3: (1sc, inc) x6 [18]

Rnd 4: (2sc, inc) x6 [24]

Rnd 5–Rnd 9: 24sc [24]

Rnd 10: (2sc, dec) x6 [18]

Place eyes between rnds 7 and 8, roughly 5 stitches apart. Embroider a mouth between the eyes (see page 28 for instructions). Begin to stuff.

Rnd 11: (1sc, dec) x6 [12]

Rnd 12: 6dec [6]

Fasten off and seal hole (see page 35 for instructions).

STALK

In brown

Rnd 1: Ch 5 [5]

Rnd 2: Skip first stitch, 4sc [4]

Fasten off and leave a long tail for sewing. Sew one side of the stalk between rnds 1 and 2 of the apple, and sew the other side of the stalk on the other side of the mc made in the apple, between rnds 1 and 2. Make sure that the flat part of the stalk is facing the same side that the eyes and mouth are on.

LEAF

In green

Rnd 1: Ch 4 [4]

Rnd 2: Skip first stitch, 1slst, 1sc, 1hdc [3]

Fasten off and leave a long tail for sewing. Sew the leaf in place next to the stalk in whatever position you desire.

BFF CHERRIES

Moving on, we have a cute set of BFF cherries. This gives you another chance to practice making a basic ball—but this time, a little smaller. This is a great way to practice tiny details so you can get used to smaller projects. (Though they may seem fiddly, they are still on the beginner level!)

CHERRY BODY X2
Starting at the top
In red

Rnd 1: 6sc into mc [6]

Rnd 2: 6inc [12]

Rnd 3: (1sc, inc) x6 [18]

Rnd 4–Rnd 6: 18sc [18]

Rnd 7: (1sc, dec) x6 [12]

Place eyes between rnds 5 and 6, roughly 3 stitches apart. Embroider a mouth between the eyes (see page 28 for instructions). Begin to stuff.

Rnd 8: 6dec [6]

Fasten off and seal hole (see page 35 for instructions).

CHERRY STALK X2
In green

Rnd 1: Ch 6 [6]

Fasten off and leave a long tail for sewing. Attach your embroidery needle to the tail of one stalk, and then sew two of the stalk ends together at an angle to make a V shape. Sew the other ends of the stalks to the cherries (one for each cherry). They should be sewn through the starting mc of the cherry (rnd 1 of the cherry body).

LEAF
In green

Rnd 1: Ch 6 [6]

Rnd 2: Skip 2 stitches, slst, 1sc, 1hdc, 1dc [4]

Fasten off and leave a long tail for sewing. Sew the leaf to the top of the stalk in whatever position you desire.

STRAWBERRY

With this lovable Strawberry, you'll start to learn how to shape your crochet. The Strawberry project is also a great time to get comfortable practicing some sewing when you add the seeds in yellow yarn.

STRAWBERRY BODY
Starting at the top
In red

Rnd 1: 6sc into mc [6]

Rnd 2: 6inc [12]

Rnd 3: (1sc, inc) x6 [18]

Rnd 4: (2sc, inc) x6 [24]

Rnd 5–Rnd 8: 24sc [24]

Rnd 9: (4sc, dec) x4 [20]

Rnd 10: 20sc [20]

Place eyes between rnds 5 and 6, roughly 5 stitches apart. Embroider a mouth between the eyes (see page 28 for instructions).

Rnd 11: (3sc, dec) x4 [16]

Begin to stuff the strawberry.

Rnd 12: 16sc [16]

Rnd 13: (2sc, dec) x4 [12]

Rnd 14: 6dec [6]

Fasten off and seal hole (see page 35 for instructions).

Using light-yellow yarn, sew small stitches around the strawberry to create seeds.

LEAVES
In green

Rnd 1: 6sc into mc [6]

Rnd 2: 6inc [12]

Rnd 3: (Ch 4, skip first stitch of ch – slst, 1hdc, 1dc – now working back into the main crochet, 2slst) x6 [12]

Fasten off and leave a long tail for sewing. Align the mc of the leaves with the mc of the strawberry, and sew the leaves into place. Sew down the rest of the strawberry, but make sure that some of the leaves are poking out still.

STEM
In green

Rnd 1: Ch 4 [4]

Rnd 2: Skip first stitch, 3sc [3]

Fasten off and leave a long tail for sewing. Sew each side of the bottom of the stem around the mc of the leaves to ensure that the stem is secure.

ICE CREAM

Time for a super-cute kawaii Ice Cream: a scoop in a cone. Now is your chance to learn something new. The ice cream "drips" are an opportunity to try out the FLO and BLO stitches described earlier in the Beginners' Techniques section (page 15). These are key techniques to learn since they help you create adorable details.

SCOOP AND CONE
Starting at the top
In white

Rnd 1: 6sc into mc [6]

Rnd 2: 6inc [12]

Rnd 3: (1sc, inc) x6 [18]

Rnd 4: (2sc, inc) x6 [24]

Rnd 5–Rnd 8: 24sc [24]

Rnd 9: In FLO, (1hdc, 1dc, and 1hdc into same stitch, slst) x8 [32]

Change color to brown (see page 43 for instructions).

Rnd 10: In the BLO of the last rnd, 24sc [24]

Rnd 11: (2sc, dec) x6 [18]

Place eyes between rnds 6 and 7, roughly 4 or 5 stitches apart. Embroider a mouth between the eyes (see page 28 for instructions).

Rnd 12–Rnd 13: 18sc [18]

Rnd 14: (1sc, dec) x6 [12]

Begin to stuff the ice cream. Make sure to be continuously stuffing from now on.

Rnd 15–Rnd 16: 12sc [12]

Rnd 17: 6dec [6]

Fasten off and seal hole (see page 35 for instructions).

Sew some sprinkles around the ice cream, using different colors of yarn.

PINEAPPLE

How about this lovely little guy—the Pineapple? This project allows you to practice your chevron sewing stitch (the V shape). As we've mentioned, when you are crocheting amigurumi minis, being able to sew confidently can make all the difference. So, enjoy the process and have fun!

PINEAPPLE BODY

Starting at the top
In yellow

Rnd 1: 6sc into mc [6]

Rnd 2: 6inc [12]

Rnd 3: (1sc, inc) x6 [18]

Rnd 4: (2sc, inc) x6 [24]

Rnd 5–Rnd 11: 24sc [24]

Rnd 12: (2sc, dec) x6 [18]

Place eyes between rnds 5 and 6, roughly 4 to 5 stitches apart. Embroider a mouth between the eyes (see page 28 for instructions).

Rnd 13: (1sc, dec) x6 [12]

Rnd 14: 6dec [6]

Fasten off and seal hole (see page 35 for instructions).

SPIKES X5

In green

Rnd 1: Ch 6 [6]

Rnd 2: Skip first stitch, slst, 3sc, 1hdc [5]

Fasten off and leave a long tail for sewing. Sew four of the spikes around the mc (between rnds 1 and 2); make sure that each side of the spike is touching another spike. Sew the last spike in the middle of the ring made with the four spikes. Make sure that the flat side of the spike is facing forward on the side where the face is.

Using orange yarn, sew V-shaped stitches around the body to create the prickles of the pineapple. Create the V shapes by sewing two diagonal running stitches between two rnds of the body.

BFF PEAS IN A POD

Here's another lovely BFF project—the Peas in a Pod! We love these cuties, and it is time to learn something new! In this pattern, you will have to work on the other side of the chain (see the Useful Techniques section on page 35). To challenge yourself even further, you could even adapt the pattern to have three BFF peas instead of two!

PEAS X2
Starting at the top
In light green

Rnd 1: 6sc into mc [6]

Rnd 2: 6inc [12]

Rnd 3-Rnd 5: 12sc [12]

Place eyes between rnds 4 and 5, roughly 3 stitches apart. Embroider a mouth between the eyes (see page 28 for instructions).

Rnd 6: 6dec [6]

Stuff.

Fasten off and seal hole (see page 35 for instructions).

POD
In dark green

Rnd 1: Ch 20 [20]

Rnd 2: Skip first stitch, 2sc, 1hdc, 13dc, 1hdc, 2sc, now working on the other side of the ch (see page 38 for instructions), 2sc, 1hdc, 13dc, 1hdc, 2sc [38]

Rnd 3: 2sc, 15hdc, 4sc, 15hdc, 2sc [38]

Rnd 4: 38sc [38]

You may need to add fewer or more rnds to the pod, depending on the size and quantity of your peas.

Fasten off and leave a long tail for sewing. Position the peas in the pod however you like. You may need to tug the pod over the peas and pin everything into place. Sew the pod into position around the peas. (You will have to sew it directly to the peas because otherwise the peas will fall out.)

Pinch the spare spaces on the outside of the peas, and sew the two edges closed to give you the pointy sides of the pod.

The **BIG BOOK** of **BEGINNER AMIGURUMI**

CANDY CORN

Time for our Candy Corn dude, as we start to add some extra shapes to our amigurumi. Our candy corn dude has some quirky little legs that give him such a great personality. This is a chance to practice something slightly fiddlier as you practice getting that perfect shape of the legs!

CANDY CORN BODY

Starting at the top
In white

Rnd 1: 6sc into mc [6]

Rnd 2: 6sc [6]

Rnd 3: (1sc, inc) x3 [9]

Rnd 4: (2sc, inc) x3 [12]

Change color to orange (see page 43 for instructions).

Rnd 5: (3sc, inc) x3 [15]

Rnd 6–Rnd 7: 15sc [15]

Rnd 8: (4sc, inc) x3 [18]

Place eyes between rnds 6 and 7, roughly 3 to 4 stitches apart. Embroider a mouth between the eyes (see page 28 for instructions).

Change color to yellow (see page 43 for instructions).

Rnd 9: 18sc [18]

Rnd 10: (5sc, inc) x3 [21]

Rnd 11: 21sc [21]

Rnd 12: (5sc, dec) x3 [18]

Rnd 13: (1sc, dec) x6 [12]

Rnd 14: 6dec [6]

Fasten off and seal hole (see page 35 for instructions).

LEGS X2

In yellow

Rnd 1: 6sc into mc [6]

Rnd 2: (1sc, inc) x3 [9]

Rnd 3: 9sc [9]

Rnd 4: 2sc, 3dec, 1sc [6]

Rnd 5–Rnd 6: 6sc [6]

Fasten off and leave a long tail for sewing. Place legs between rnds 12 and 13. They should be directly in line with the eyes. Sew the legs in place.

BY the SEASIDE

What better place is there than the seaside? These fun and cute projects are still easy, but you will have a chance to try a larger variety of different stitches and techniques.

In this section, we will take a look at some of the most popular amigurumi out there, including the classics that everyone loves to make: the Whale (page 63), the Turtle (page 71), and the Jellyfish (page 64). These popular projects are quick to crochet, and if you love to make and sell or give away your creations, you won't go wrong with these—especially if you use plush yarn!

Once you have mastered these favorites, we challenge you to stretch out of your comfort zone a little bit more. You will learn how to join two pieces of crochet with the Starfish (page 68), create more complex shapes with the Seagull (page 72), and finish off with yet another popular make—your first amigurumi doll— the Mermaid (page 75)!

WHALE

We start this section off with the Whale. The Whale is considered to be a go-to project for beginners—one up from crocheting your ball-shaped Apple (page 47). It not only allows you to experience the color change, but also to start incorporating new stitches, such as the half double crochet for fins and flippers.

WHALE BODY
Starting at the top of the head
In blue

Rnd 1: 6sc into mc [6]

Rnd 2: 6inc [12]

Rnd 3: (1sc, inc) x6 [18]

Rnd 4: (2sc, inc) x6 [24]

Rnd 5–Rnd 7: 24sc [24]

Rnd 8: 1sc, (now we are making the tail) ch 5 - skip 2 stitches of ch, 2hdc, 1sc down ch – slst into the main crochet, ch 5 - skip 2 stitches of ch, 2hdc, 1sc down ch - slst back into the same stitch of the main crochet, 5sc, (now we are making the fins) ch 4 – skip first stitch of ch, slst, 1sc, 1hdc down the ch – 13sc into the main crochet, ch 4 – skip first stitch of ch, slst, 1sc, 1hdc down the ch – 4sc into main body [37]

Change color to white (see page 43 for instructions).

Rnd 9: In BLO, 24sc (make sure when you are going around, you skip where we have made the tail and fins: don't go into the chains made last rnd) [24]

Rnd 10: (2sc, dec) x6 [18]

Place eyes between rnds 7 and 8, roughly 6 stitches apart. Embroider a mouth between the eyes (see page 28 for instructions).

Begin to stuff the whale.

Rnd 11: (1sc, dec) x6 [12]

Rnd 12: 6dec [6]

Fasten off and seal hole (see page 35 for instructions).

JELLYFISH

Another beginner favorite is the Jelly-fish. Jellyfish are super-cute projects that are ideal for ANY colored yarn—especially yarn scraps, as they look great in multiple colors. This adorable pattern will not only test your skills at FLO and BLO but also help build your confidence with harder stitches such as a double crochet.

This project was made using a multicolored ball of yarn—so no color changes are needed. It will look adorable in single colors, too!

JELLYFISH BODY
Starting at the top of the head

Rnd 1: 6sc into mc [6]

Rnd 2: 6inc [12]

Rnd 3: (1sc, inc) x6 [18]

Rnd 4: (2sc, inc) x6 [24]

Rnd 5–Rnd 8: 24sc [24]

Rnd 9: In FLO, (1hdc, 1dc, and 1hdc into the same stitch, 2slst) x6 [30]

Rnd 10: In BLO of the last rnd, (2sc, dec) x6 [18]

Place eyes between rnds 6 and 7, roughly 5 stitches apart. Embroider a mouth between the eyes (see page 28 for instructions).

Begin to stuff the jellyfish.

Rnd 11: (1sc, dec) x6 [12]

Rnd 12: 6dec [6]

Fasten off and seal hole (see page 35 for instructions).

TENDRILS X2

Rnd 1: Ch 47 [47]

Fasten off and leave a medium-length tail.

Thread one of the tendrils (chains) through an embroidery needle. On the base of the jellyfish, push the needle through the side and underneath the final ring-shaped rnd of the body (rnd 12). Then push the needle out to the other side. Pull the needle so you have the tentacle threaded through the body. This should now look like there are two tendrils. Pull one side, so it is even to the other side. Repeat this with the other tentacle (chain).

Cut two pieces of yarn, equal in length to the ch 47. Repeat instructions for attaching the tendrils.

CRAB

Let's make a mini Crab. This Crab is fun, it's quick to make, and it's a great way to use up any leftover scraps of red, orange, or pink yarn you may have left over from your previous projects. It will also allow you to practice your sewing skills!

CRAB BODY
Starting with the top of the head/shell

Rnd 1: 6sc into mc [6]

Rnd 2: 6inc [12]

Rnd 3: (1sc, inc) x6 [18]

Rnd 4: (2sc, inc) x6 [24]

Rnd 5: 24sc [24]

Rnd 6: In BLO, (2sc, dec) x6 [18]

Place eyes between rnds 4 and 5, roughly 3 to 4 stitches apart. Embroider a mouth between the eyes (see page 28 for instructions).

Rnd 7: (1sc, dec) x6 [12]

Stuff.

Rnd 8: 6dec [6]

Fasten off and seal hole (see page 35 for instructions).

CLAWS X2

Rnd 1: Ch 8 [8]

Rnd 2: Skip first stitch, 3slst, ch 4 – 3slst down the ch – slst back into the same stitch, 4slst [11]

Fasten off and leave a long tail for sewing. Sew the claws on each side of the eyes, between rnds 5 and 6 (underneath the rim made from the BLO).

LEGS X6

Rnd 1: Ch 5 [5]

Rnd 2: Skip first stitch, 4slst [4]

Fasten off and leave a long tail for sewing. Sew three legs on each side of the body. They should be in line with the claws, and each leg should be positioned directly next to each other, with no gaps.

STARFISH

It's time to learn something new whilst making this next project. We love the Starfish because it is so very happy. This project actually requires very little sewing, but it challenges you to learn how to crochet two sides together and work on the other side of a chain. Be patient with this project; we promise that you will love the results!

STARFISH BODY X2

Starting with the middle of the starfish

Rnd 1: 8sc into mc [8]

Rnd 2: (1sc, inc) x4 [12]

Rnd 3: (3sc, inc) x3 [15]

Rnd 4: 1sc, ch 6 – skip first stitch, 5sc down the ch –, (3sc back into the main crochet, ch 6 – skip first stitch, 5sc down the ch –) x3, 3sc, ch 6 – skip first stitch, 5sc down the ch –, 2sc back into the main body [35]

Rnd 5: 1sc, (into the side of ch, 5sc, working on the other side of the ch [see page 38 for instructions], 5sc (1sc in each stitch), 3sc into the main crochet) x5, 2sc [65]

Place eyes roughly between rnds 2 and 3, on each side of the mc. Embroider a mouth between the eyes (see page 28 for instructions). Only place eyes onto one of the starfish sides—not both.

Now that you have two flat star shapes, crochet together the two sides (see page 36 for instructions). Make sure that the backs are on the inside of your work. Crochet ¾ of the way around and stuff the starfish. Finish crocheting the two sides together. Sew in tail end of yarn.

TURTLE

We love this Turtle project, which is destined to be a bestseller for anyone hosting a market stall. You can really have fun with the colors, too. The pattern, once again, is super-basic and easy—though it does include crocheting two sides together again, plus a bit of sewing!

SHELL
Starting at the top
In brown

Rnd 1: 6sc into mc [6]

Rnd 2: 6inc [12]

Rnd 3: (1sc, inc) x6 [18]

Rnd 4: (2sc, inc) x6 [24]

Rnd 5–Rnd 6: 24sc [24]

Rnd 7: In FLO, 24sc [24]

Change color to green (see page 43 for instructions).

Rnd 8: In the BLO of the last rnd, (2sc, dec) x6 [18]

Begin to stuff the shell.

Rnd 9: (1sc, dec) x6 [12]

Rnd 10: 6dec [6]

Fasten off and seal hole (see page 35 for instructions).

HEAD
Starting at the front of the face
In green

Rnd 1: 6sc into mc [6]

Rnd 2: 6inc [12]

Rnd 3: (3sc, inc) x3 [15]

Rnd 4: 15sc [15]

Rnd 5: (3sc, dec) x3 [12]

Place eyes roughly between rnds 2 and 3 (this may have to vary), on each side of the mc (rnd 1). Embroider a mouth between the eyes (see page 28 for instructions). Stuff.

Fasten off and leave a long tail for sewing. Do not seal the hole. Sew the head to the shell. The bottom of the head should be in line with the bottom of the brown part of the shell. The top of the head should be roughly between rnds 3 and 4 of the shell.

FINS X4
In green

Rnd 1: 6sc into mc [6]

Rnd 2: 6inc [12]

Fold in half, and crochet together the sides (see page 36 for instructions) to create a semicircle.

Fasten off and leave a long tail for sewing. Put the shell on its back, so the green stomach is facing upward. Sew a fin onto each corner of the body. The fins should be sewn roughly between rnds 7 and 8. Make sure that all the fins are facing the correct way.

SEAGULL

Every seaside needs a Seagull! We think this little guy is quite mischievous and may get into all sorts of trouble. The Seagull has a lovely shaped body, which shows you the magic of how crochet allows you to create all kinds of shapes for your designs. This is another great pattern for sewing practice and learning new stitches!

SEAGULL BODY
Starting with the top of the head
In white

Rnd 1: 6sc into mc [6]

Rnd 2: 6inc [12]

Rnd 3: (1sc, inc) x6 [18]

Rnd 4–Rnd 8: 18sc [18]

Rnd 9: 3sc, 5inc, 5sc, 3inc, 2sc [26]

Rnd 10: 6sc, 4hdc inc, 16sc [30]

Place eyes between rnds 4 and 5, roughly 4 stitches apart. The eyes should be on the other side of where the hdcs have been made (the hdcs are the back of the seagull to form the tail). Stuff the head.

Rnd 11–Rnd 13: 30sc [30]

Rnd 14: (3sc, dec) x6 [24]

Rnd 15: (2sc, dec) x6 [18]

Begin to stuff the body.

Rnd 16: (1sc, dec) x6 [12]

Rnd 17: 6dec [6]

Fasten off and seal hole (see page 35 for instructions).

WINGS X2
In grey

Rnd 1: Into mc, ch 1, 7dc [7]

Change color to black (see page 43 for instructions).

Rnd 2: Ch 1 and turn, 7sc, 1sc into the ch that was made at the beginning of the first rnd [8]

Fasten off and leave a long tail for sewing. Sew one wing on each side of the body. The top of the wing should be positioned diagonally in line with the eye, and it should be sewn between rnds 8 and 9. The bottom of the wing should be sewn between rnds 11 and 12. Sew the rest of the wing in place, to ensure it won't come off.

(continued)

BEAK

In yellow

Rnd 1: Ch 4 [4]

Rnd 2: Skip first stitch, 1slst, 1sc, 1hdc [3]

Fasten off and leave a long tail for sewing. You should have made a long triangle shape. Sew the beak between rnds 4 and 5, directly between the eyes.

LEGS X2

In yellow

Rnd 1: Ch 10 [10]

Rnd 2: Skip first stitch, 2slst, (ch 3 – Skip first stitch and 2slst down the ch – slst into same stitch of the main crochet) x2, 7slst [15]

Fasten off and leave a long tail for sewing. Sew each leg to the base of the seagull, roughly between rnds 14 and 15. The legs should be in line with the eyes.

MERMAID DOLL

It's time to learn to make a simple doll! Here we start you off with the Mermaid—a popular project to make, gift, or sell. One of the most challenging parts of all amigurumi dolls is often the hair, which usually requires a lot of extra crochet and yarn supplies, so we've created a method that is relatively simple and doesn't use too much yarn, either. With this fun project, not only will you learn to make hair, but you will also increase your crochet skills as you crochet the tail, which requires a combination of different techniques.

TAIL AND BODY
Starting with the tail
In tail color (e.g., turquoise, pink, or purple)

Rnd 1: 6sc into mc [6]

Rnd 2: 6sc [6]

Rnd 3: (1sc, inc) x3 [9]

Rnd 4: 9sc [9]

Rnd 5: (2sc, inc) x3 [12]

Rnd 6: 12sc [12]

Rnd 7: (3sc, inc) x3 [15]

Rnd 8–Rnd 9: 15sc [15]

Rnd 10: 5sc, inc, 9sc [16]

Rnd 11: 16sc [16]

Rnd 12: 16hdc [16]

Change color to skin tone (see page 43 for instructions).

Rnd 13: In the very BLO of the last rnd (the third loop of the hdcs), 2sc, dec (the dec should be on the hip of the doll, so you may need to change its placement), 6sc, dec (the dec should be on the hip of the doll again), 4sc [14]

Stuff the tail.

Rnd 14: 14sc [14]

Change color to mermaid top color (e.g., purple).

Rnd 15: 14sc [14]

Rnd 16: (5sc, dec) x2 [12]

Change color to skin tone.

Rnd 17: 6dec [6]

Stuff.

(continued)

MERMAID DOLL (CONTINUED)

HEAD

Carrying on from the body
In skin tone

Rnd 18: 6inc [12]

Rnd 19: (1sc, inc) x6 [18]

Rnd 20: (2sc, inc) x6 [24]

Rnd 21-Rnd 25: 24sc [24]

Place eyes between rnds 22 and 23, about 4 stitches apart.

Rnd 26: (2sc, dec) x6 [18]

Begin to stuff the head.

Rnd 27: (1sc, dec) x6 [12]

Continue to stuff.

Rnd 28: 6dec [6]

Fasten off and seal the hole (see page 35 for instructions).

ARMS X2

In skin color

Rnd 1: 5sc into mc [5]

Rnd 2-Rnd 7: 5sc [5]

Fasten off and leave a long tail for sewing.

Sew arms between rnds 15 and 16, placing one arm on each side of the doll. (You may need to change the positioning to suit your doll accordingly.)

FINS

In tail color or color of choice (e.g., turquoise, pink, or purple)

Rnd 1: Ch 6 [6]

Rnd 2: Skip 2 stitches, 4hdc, working on the other side of the ch (see page 38 for instructions), 4hdc, ch 6, skip 2 stitches of the ch, 4hdc into the ch, on the other side of the ch, 4hdc, slst into same stitch [16]

Fasten off and leave a long tail for sewing. Sew the two fins together slightly, so they stay next to each other in position. Sew each end of the fins roughly between rnds 2 and 3, on each side of the mc made in the first rnd of the tail, making sure they are secure.

HAIR

For instructions, see How to Sew on Hair (page 33).

STARFISH HAIR ACCESSORY

In color of choice (e.g., light green)

Rnd 1: Into mc, (ch 3 - skip first of the ch, slst, sc, down the ch - slst into the mc) x5 [15]

Fasten off and leave a long tail for sewing. Sew the starfish to the side of the head, as an accessory. You can also sew it to other places of the doll in a position of your choice.

IN the GARDEN

The majority of patterns in this book use a limited number of rounds, so you can complete each project quite quickly. That means you get instant gratification and have fewer unfinished projects taking up your craft space. We start off super-easy in this garden-themed section with another firm favorite for all new amigurumi makers: the Bumble Bee (page 81)! We also have many other cute little patterns for you—and they make lovely spring projects, too!

BUMBLE BEE

First up we have a terrific Bumble Bee. This is another wonderful classic that many beginners love to make. It offers a great chance to practice your color changing, and you will need to position the face in the correct place so the color change is less noticeable at the base. The Bumble Bee is popular as a keychain, and it is also a bestseller at market stalls in a plush yarn.

BEE BODY
Starting with the front of the face
In yellow

Rnd 1: 6sc into mc [6]

Rnd 2: 6inc [12]

Rnd 3: (1sc, inc) x6 [18]

Rnd 4: (2sc, inc) x6 [24]

Rnd 5: 24sc [24]

Change color to black (see page 43 for instructions).

Rnd 6-Rnd 7: 24sc [24]

Change color to yellow.

Rnd 8-Rnd 9: 24sc [24]

Change color to black.

Rnd 10-Rnd 11: 24sc [24]

Place eyes between rnds 3 and 4, on each side of the mc (rnd 1). (This may have to vary to suit your bee. Also ensure that the positioning of the color change is turned to the bottom of the bee.) Embroider a mouth between the eyes (see page 28 for instructions).

Change color to yellow.

Rnd 12: (2sc, dec) x6 [18]

Stuff.

Rnd 13: (1sc, dec) x6 [12]

Rnd 14: 6 dec [6]

Fasten off and seal hole (see page 35 for instructions).

WINGS X2
In white

Rnd 1: Into mc, ch 2, 7dc, slst into the first dc of the rnd [7]

Fasten off and leave a long tail for sewing. Sew each wing between rnds 8 and 9, roughly 2 or 3 stitches apart.

SUNFLOWER

Next, we make a pretty Sunflower—a quick project to use up some leftover bits and pieces of yarn. This Sunflower would also make an adorable pin! Just remember to be patient and take your time when adding the petals. We recommend using pins to hold them into place while you are sewing.

CENTER OF THE FLOWER

Starting with the front of the flower face
In brown

Rnd 1: 6sc into mc [6]

Rnd 2: 6inc [12]

Rnd 3: (1sc, inc) x6 [18]

Rnd 4–Rnd 5: 18sc [18]

Place eyes between rnds 2 and 3, on each side of the mc. Embroider a mouth between the eyes (see page 28 for instructions). Begin to stuff.

Rnd 6: (1sc, dec) x6 [12]

Rnd 7: 6dec [6]

Fasten off and seal hole (see page 35 for instructions).

PETALS

In yellow

Rnd 1: Ch 26 [26]

Rnd 2: Skip first stitch, 1slst, (ch 5 – skip first stitch of the ch, 2slst, 1sc, 1hdc down the ch –, 2slst) x12 [73]

Fasten off and leave a long tail for sewing. Wrap the petals all the way around the head of the flower. They should be sewn between rnds 4 and 5.

SNAIL

Let's make a cute little Snail. Here we have more fun with color changes, and you get to practice crocheting together two sides and shaping your amigurumi to give it the perfect finish.

SHELL
Starting with the center of the shell
In turquoise

Rnd 1: 6sc into mc [6]

Rnd 2: 6inc [12]

Rnd 3: Change color to light blue (see page 43 for instructions), (1sc, inc) x6 [18]

Rnd 4: (2sc, inc) x6 [24]

Rnd 5–Rnd 6: Change color to turquoise, 24sc [24]

Rnd 7–Rnd 8: Change color to light blue, 24sc [24]

Rnd 9: Change color to turquoise, (2sc, dec) x6 [18]

Stuff.

Rnd 10: (1sc, dec) x6 [12]

Rnd 11: Change color to light blue, 6dec [6]

Fasten off and seal hole (see page 35 for instructions).

SNAIL BODY
Starting at the top of the head
In white

Rnd 1: 6sc into mc [6]

Rnd 2: 6inc [12]

Rnd 3: (1sc, inc) x6 [18]

Rnd 4–Rnd 11: 18sc [18]

Fold head in half, and place eyes between rnds 4 and 5, roughly 3 to 4 stitches apart. Make sure that each eye is placed on each side of the fold. Embroider a mouth between the eyes (see page 28 for instructions). Stuff.

Rnd 12: Crochet together the two sides of the head (see page 36 for instructions), 8sc across [8]

Rnd 13–Rnd 19: Ch 1 and turn, 8sc [8]

Fasten off and leave a long tail for sewing. Line up the head against the shell, with half of the head sticking out above the top of the shell, and the eyes facing to the side. Sew into place. Wrap the body along the base of the shell and sew into place.

ANTENNAE X2
In the snail's body color (e.g., white)

Rnd 1: Ch 4 [4]

Rnd 2: Skip first stitch, 3sc [3]

Fasten off and leave a long tail for sewing. Sew one edge of the antenna between rnds 1 and 2, and the other side between rnds 2 and 3. Repeat for the other antenna. Make sure that both antennae are sewn directly above and in line with the eyes.

FROG

We love making this Frog! The pattern works really well for a plushie if you use a chunky yarn. This Frog is one of the bigger projects in this book. Plan for it to take a bit longer than most of the other projects, since you must crochet more rounds and work with more stitches.

FROG BODY
Starting with the top of the head
In green

Rnd 1: 6sc into mc [6]

Rnd 2: 6inc [12]

Rnd 3: (1sc, inc) x6 [18]

Rnd 4: (2sc, inc) x6 [24]

Rnd 5–Rnd 9: 24sc [24]

Rnd 10: (2sc, dec) x6 [18]

Stuff.

Rnd 11: In FLO, (2sc, inc) x6 [24]

Rnd 12–Rnd 15: 24sc [24]

Rnd 16: (2sc, dec) x6 [18]

Stuff.

Rnd 17: (1sc, dec) x6 [12]

Rnd 18: 6dec [6]

Fasten off and seal hole (see page 35 for instructions).

EYES X2
In green

Rnd 1: 6sc into mc [6]

Rnd 2: (1sc, inc) x3 [9]

Rnd 3–Rnd 4: 9sc [9]

Fasten off and leave a long tail for sewing. Place a safety eye between rnds 3 and 4, in both eyes. Sew the top of the eye roughly between rnds 2 and 3 (this may have to vary), and sew the bottom of the eye between rnds 5 and 6. Do the same for the other eye. Embroider a mouth between the eyes (see page 28 for instructions).

(continued)

FROG (CONTINUED)

FEET X2

In green

Rnd 1: 6sc into mc [6]

Rnd 2: 6inc [12]

Rnd 3-Rnd 4: 12sc [12]

Fasten off and leave a long tail for sewing. Stuff foot lightly. Sew the feet to the body, directly underneath the eyes. The top of the foot should be sewn roughly between rnds 14 and 15, and the bottom of the foot should be sewn roughly between rnds 17 and 18 (this may have to vary). Sew the rest of the foot on to ensure that it is attached securely.

ARMS X2

In green

Rnd 1: 6sc into mc [6]

Rnd 2-Rnd 5: 6sc [6]

Fasten off and leave a long tail for sewing. Sew the top of the arm between rnds 10 and 11. Move the hand so it appears to be resting on the frog's belly. Sew into position. Make sure to do this for both hands.

BUTTERFLY

Every garden needs a Butterfly. This fun project uses up different odds and ends of yarn, whilst stretching your ability to practice different shapes, stitches, and techniques.

BUTTERFLY BODY
Starting with the top of the head
In pink

Rnd 1: 6sc into mc [6]

Rnd 2: 6inc [12]

Rnd 3: (1sc, inc) x6 [18]

Rnd 4–Rnd 6: 18sc [18]

Rnd 7: (1sc, dec) x6 [12]

Rnd 8: In FLO, (1sc, inc) x6 [18]

Place eyes between rnds 5 and 6, 5 stitches apart. Embroider a mouth between the eyes (see page 28 for instructions).

Rnd 9–Rnd 11: 18sc [18]

Begin to stuff.

Rnd 12: (1sc, dec) x6 [12]

Rnd 13: 6dec [6]

Fasten off and seal hole (see page 35 for instructions).

ANTENNAE X2
In pink

Rnd 1: Ch 4 [4]

Rnd 2: Skip first stitch, 3slst [3]

Fasten off and leave a long tail for sewing. Sew one side of an antenna between rnds 2 and 3 of the body and the other side between rnds 3 and 4. It should be directly in line with one of the eyes. Repeat for the other antenna.

LARGE WINGS X2
In purple

Rnd 1: Ch 12 [12]

Rnd 2: Skip 2 stitches, 1slst, 1sc, 8dc, ch 1, now working on the other side of the ch (see page 38 for instructions), 8dc, 1sc, 1slst [20]

Fasten off and leave a long tail for sewing. Sew one edge of the bottom of a wing between rnds 6 and 7 of the body, and the other edge between rnds 9 and 10. Make sure that it is on the back of the butterfly. Allow for most of the wing to be seen from the front of the butterfly. Repeat for the other wing. Make sure that the wings are around 3 to 4 stitches apart. You can also sew them on at a slight angle to make sure that the wings don't stick out unnaturally straight.

(continued)

BUTTERFLY (CONTINUED)

SMALL WINGS X2

In blue

Rnd 1: Ch 8 [8]

Rnd 2: Skip 2 stitches, 1slst, 1sc, 4dc, ch 1, now working on the other side of the ch, 4dc, 1sc, 1slst [12]

Fasten off and leave a long tail for sewing. Sew one edge of the bottom of a wing between rnds 9 and 10 of the body, and the other edge between rnds 11 and 12. Make sure that it is on the back of the butterfly. Allow for most of the wing to be seen from the front of the butterfly. Repeat for the other wing. Make sure that the wings are around 4 to 5 stitches apart. You can also sew them on at a slight angle to make sure that the wings don't stick out unnaturally straight. They should be directly below the large wings.

CACTUS AND PLANT POT

Another popular beginner crochet theme is the Cactus! Here we show you how to make a Cactus with a separate Plant Pot. The Plant Pot is a great base for both the cactus and the flower buddies. The Egg in the Farm section (page 101) also loves to sit in it! This is a chance to make a multiple-part project and create a whole amigurumi using only double crochet rather than single crochet.

PLANT POT
Starting at the bottom of the plant pot
In brown

Rnd 1: 6sc into mc [6]

Rnd 2: 6 inc [12]

Rnd 3: (1sc, inc) x6 [18]

Rnd 4: (2sc, inc) x6 [24]

Rnd 5: In BLO, 24sc [24]

Rnd 6–Rnd 9: 24sc [24]

Rnd 10: Ch 2, in FLO, 24dc, slst between the first dc and the ch [24]

Fasten off and leave a medium-length tail. Weave in the tail. Fold over the last row of dc outward, so a rim for the plant pot is made.

Optional: Trace the base of the plant pot on some card and cut it out. Put the cardboard into the base of the plant pot, to give it more stability.

CACTUS BODY
Starting with the top of the cactus
In green

Rnd 1: 6dc into mc [6]

Rnd 2: 6dc inc [12]

Rnd 3: (1dc, dc inc) x6 [18]

Rnd 4: (2dc, dc inc) x6 [24]

Rnd 5: 24dc [24]

Rnd 6: (2dc, dc dec) x6 [18]

Place eyes in the middle of rnd 3, roughly 4 stitches apart. Sew a straight line between the eyes to create the mouth.

Rnd 7: (1dc, dc dec) x6 [12]

Stuff.

Rnd 8: 6dec [6] (the decrease here should be a single crochet decrease)

(continued)

Fasten off and seal hole (see page 35 for instructions).

Using white thread, embroider little lines around the cactus, to give it spikes.

ARMS X2

In green

Rnd 1: 6sc into mc [6]

Rnd 2-Rnd 4: 6sc [6]

Fasten off and leave a long tail for sewing. Sew the top of the arms on each side of the body, roughly between rnds 4 and 5. Move the hand slightly, so it appears to be resting on the plant's stomach, and sew it into place. Make sure to do this for both hands.

BIG FLOWER

In light pink

Rnd 1: 5sc into mc [5]

Rnd 2: (ch 6, skip 2 stitches of the ch – 1hdc, 3dc down the ch – now working into the main crochet, slst) x5 [20]

Fasten off and leave a long tail for sewing. Align the mc of the flower with the mc of the cactus; sew into place. Sew around the rest of the flower, making sure that some of the petals still stick out.

SMALL FLOWER

In light pink

Rnd 1: Into mc, (ch 4, skip first stitch of the ch - 2sc, hdc down the ch – now working into the mc again, slst) x5 [20]

Fasten off and leave a long tail for sewing. Align the middle of the flower with the mc of the big flower; sew into place. Sew down the rest of the flower, making sure that some of the petals are still sticking out.

SPRING FLOWER AND PLANT POT

Last but not least, in our garden section fun, we have the happy Spring Flower (and pot). The flower simply makes us smile! This amigurumi, which is also a little bit bigger, provides the perfect opportunity to show off your knowledge of different stitches and your capability to sew on a variety of details.

PLANT POT

Follow the same directions for the plant pot included in the Cactus and Plant Pot pattern (page 92).

FLOWER BODY
Starting with the top of the head
In yellow

Rnd 1: 6sc into mc [6]

Rnd 2: 6inc [12]

Rnd 3: (1sc, inc) x6 [18]

Rnd 4: (2sc, inc) x6 [24]

Rnd 5: (3sc, inc) x6 [30]

Rnd 6–Rnd 10: 30sc [30]

Rnd 11: (3sc, dec) x6 [24]

Place eyes between rnds 8 and 9, roughly 5 stitches apart. Embroider a mouth between the two eyes (see page 28 for instructions).

Rnd 12: (2sc, dec) x6 [18]

Stuff.

Change color to green (see page 43 for instructions).

Rnd 13: In FLO, (2sc, inc) x6 [24]

Rnd 14–Rnd 17: 24sc [24]

Rnd 18: (2sc, dec) x6 [18]

Stuff.

Rnd 19: (1sc, dec) x6 [12]

Rnd 20: 6dec [6]

Fasten off and seal hole (see page 35 for instructions).

(continued)

ARMS X2

In green

Rnd 1: 6sc into mc [6]

Rnd 2–Rnd 4: 6sc [6]

Fasten off and leave a long tail for sewing. Sew the top of the arms on each side of the body, roughly between rnds 12 and 13. Move the hand slightly, so it appears to be resting on its stomach; sew into place. Make sure to do this for both hands.

PETALS

In pink

Rnd 1: Ch 42 [42]

Rnd 2: Skip first stitch, 1sc, 1dc, 1tr, 1dc, (1sc, slst, 1dc, 1tr, 1dc) x7, 1sc [41]

Fasten off and leave a long tail for sewing. Hold the petals into a position where they wrap all the way around the face, without any missing gaps. You may have to pin this into position. Sew the petals onto the head, making sure that the petals are sewn all the way around.

FUN on the FARM

In this section, we will explore lots of different adorable farmyard friends and cute pets. Again, we give you a chance to have a go at some smaller and quicker projects or make something bigger, like a Bunny (page 119), which would make a great plush toy. Depending on your resources for yarn and how much time you have on hand, see how many of these patterns you can make! Remember, you can always have fun using different yarns and hooks, too.

EGG

Let's get back to basics with a super-simple Egg. You can make it plain or have fun with three different colored yarn scraps to make it into a painted egg and practice color changing. (This could also make a cute Easter tree decoration.) Alternatively, you can revisit the Food section and give it a kawaii face and maybe even some adorable little legs like the Candy Corn (page 59). The Egg also fits nicely into the Plant Pot base (page 92)!

THREE-COLORED EGG
Starting with the tip of the egg
In color A

Rnd 1: 6sc into mc [6]

Rnd 2: (1sc, inc) x3 [9]

Rnd 3: (2sc, inc) x3 [12]

Rnd 4: (3sc, inc) x3 [15]

Rnd 5: (4sc, inc) x3 [18]

Change color to B (see page 43 for instructions).

Rnd 6: (5sc, inc) x3 [21]

Change color to A.

Rnd 7: (6sc, inc) x3 [24]

Rnd 8: 24sc [24]

Change color to B.

Rnd 9: 24sc [24]

Change color to C.

Rnd 10: 24sc [24]

Change color to B.

Rnd 11: 24sc [24]

Change color to A.

Rnd 12: 24sc [24]

Rnd 13: (2sc, dec) x6 [18]

Stuff.

Rnd 14: (1sc, dec) x6 [12]

Rnd 15: 6dec [6]

Fasten off and seal hole (see page 35 for instructions).

CHICK

Once you have mastered the Egg (page 101), you can make a little Chick to keep it company. This pattern would work beautifully for a plushie, too, and you can have lots of fun with pastel spring colors, like pink, blue, or lilac. This pattern will explore different ways to shape your crochet—especially when forming the tail and using different types of stitches.

CHICK BODY
Starting with the top of the head
In yellow

Rnd 1: 6sc into mc [6]

Rnd 2: 6inc [12]

Rnd 3: (1sc, inc) x6 [18]

Rnd 4: (2sc, inc) x6 [24]

Rnd 5–Rnd 8: 24sc [24]

Rnd 9: (1sc, dec) x8 [16]

Rnd 10: (1sc, inc) x8 [24]

Rnd 11–Rnd 12: 24sc [24]

Rnd 13: 9sc, 5inc, 10sc [29]

Rnd 14: 13sc, 4hdc, 12sc [29]

Rnd 15: 29sc [29]

Place eyes between rnds 6 and 7, roughly 6 stitches apart. The eyes should be placed on the opposite side to where we have been creating the tail (the 5inc in rnd 13 and the 4hdc in rnd 14). Embroider a flat beak between the eyes (see page 29 for instructions).

Rnd 16: (1sc, dec) x9, 2sc [20]

Stuff.

Rnd 17: (1sc, dec) x6, 2sc [14]

Rnd 18: 7dec [7]

Fasten off and seal hole (see page 35 for instructions).

(continued)

CHICK (CONTINUED)

FEET X2

In orange

Rnd 1: 6sc into mc [6]

Rnd 2: 3sc, 3hdc, slst into the first stitch of the rnd [6]

Fasten off and leave a long tail for sewing. Using the bottom of the foot (where the 3sc of rnd 2 were made), sew the 3 stitches along the base of the chick, roughly between rnds 15 and 16. Make sure that the feet are pointing outward and are in line with each eye. Weave in any loose ends.

WINGS X2

In yellow

Rnd 1: 5sc into mc [5]

Rnd 2: Ch 1, 2hdc, dc, 2hdc, slst into the first stitch of the rnd [5]

Fasten off and leave a long tail for sewing. Sew the less pointed end of the wing roughly between rnds 10 and 11. The pointed end of the wing (where the dc was made) should be sewn approximately between rnds 12 and 13. Sew the rest of the wing to the body, so it is fully secured. Make sure that the wings are sewn on each side of the body.

HAPPY HEN

Of course, the Chick (page 102) will also need a mom, and the Happy Hen is just so satisfying to make. This fun pattern is one of the slightly larger projects in this section with more rounds, so plan to spend a bit longer making it!

BODY
Starting with the top of the head
In brown

Rnd 1: 6sc into mc [6]

Rnd 2: 6inc [12]

Rnd 3: (1sc, inc) x6 [18]

Rnd 4: (2sc, inc) x6 [24]

Rnd 5–Rnd 8: 24sc [24]

Rnd 9: 3sc, 4inc, 8sc, 3inc, 6sc [31]

Rnd 10: 4sc, 4hdc inc, 23sc [35]

Rnd 11: 8sc, inc, 26sc [36]

Rnd 12–Rnd 14: 36sc [36]

Place eyes between rnds 5 and 6, roughly 5 stitches apart. Sew on a beak between the eyes—two running stitches on top of each other (see page 29 for instructions).

Stuff.

Rnd 15: (4sc, dec) x6 [30]

Rnd 16: (3sc, dec) x6 [24]

Rnd 17: (2sc, dec) x6 [18]

Stuff.

Rnd 18: (1sc, dec) x6 [12]

Rnd 19: 6dec [6]

Fasten off and seal hole (see page 35 for instructions).

COMB
In red

Rnd 1: Ch 8 [8]

Rnd 2: Skip 2 stitches, dc, ch 1, slst, (ch 2, dc, ch 1, slst) x2 [6]

Fasten off and leave a long tail for sewing. Sew the front of the comb between rnds 2 and 3, and the back of the comb between rnds 3 and 4. Sew down the rest of the comb. It should go through the middle of the head, with the front of the comb in line with the middle of the eyes.

(continued)

HAPPY HEN (CONTINUED)

WATTLE

In red

Rnd 1: Ch 3 [3]

Rnd 2: Skip first stitch, 2sc, ch 3, skip first stitch of the ch 3 and 2sc down the ch [4]

Fasten off and leave a long tail for sewing. Fold the wattle in half and sew the top two sides together—this will make the two sides of the wattle slightly closer together. Sew the wattle a row under the beak (the top of the wattle should be sewn roughly between rnds 6 and 7).

WINGS X2

In brown

Rnd 1: Into mc, ch 2, 2dc, 2tr, 2dc [6]

Fasten off and leave a long tail for sewing. Sew the straight edge of the wing roughly between rnds 9 and 10. The edge of each wing should be in line with the eye.

LOAF CAT

Here we return to a basic and quick project: the super-popular Loaf Cat. Loaf Cats are always a winner at craft fairs or as gifts, and they look so cute—both in regular yarn or as a plushie!

BODY

Starting with the front of the face
In grey

Rnd 1: 6sc into mc [6]

Rnd 2: 6inc [12]

Rnd 3: (1sc, inc) x6 [18]

Rnd 4: (2sc, inc) x6 [24]

Place eyes between rnds 3 and 4, on each side of the mc. You may need to change which rnd each eye has to go in to make it look better. Embroider a nose, using pink yarn, between the eyes (see page 31 for instructions).

Rnd 5–Rnd 11: 24sc [24]

Rnd 12: (2sc, dec) x6 [18]

Begin to stuff.

Rnd 13: (1sc, dec) x6 [12]

Rnd 14: 6dec [6]

Fasten off and seal hole (see page 35 for instructions).

EARS X2

In grey

Rnd 1: Into a mc, 1sc, 2dc, 1sc [4]

Make sure that when you pull your mc closed, you have a flat side for the base of the ear.

Fasten off and leave a long tail for sewing. Place the ear between rnds 5 and 6 of the body. The bottom of the ears should be roughly in line with the eyes.

LEGS X4

In grey

Rnd 1: 6sc into mc [6]

Rnd 2: 6sc [6]

Fasten off and leave a long tail for sewing. Sew one side of a leg between rnds 4 and 5, and the other side between rnds 7 and 8 of the body. (Do this for the two front legs.) Make sure that they are in line with the eyes. For the back legs, sew one side of the leg between rnds 8 and 9 and the other side between rnds 11 and 12. Make sure that they are in line with the front legs.

TAIL

In grey

Rnd 1: Ch 7 [7]

Rnd 2: Skip first stitch, 6sc [6]

Fasten off and leave a long tail for sewing. Sew the tail between rnds 12 and 13 of the body. Make sure that it is in line with the middle of the two ears.

PUG

And, of course, we are not forgetting the dog lovers. Here you can also have a go at making a lovely little Pug. So much cuteness!

BODY
Starting with the top of the head
In beige

Rnd 1: 6sc into mc [6]

Rnd 2: 6inc [12]

Rnd 3: (1sc, inc) x6 [18]

Rnd 4: (2sc, inc) x6 [24]

Rnd 5: (3sc, inc) x6 [30]

Rnd 6–Rnd 11: 30sc [30]

Rnd 12: (3sc, dec) x6 [24]

Rnd 13: (2sc, dec) x6 [18]

Place eyes between rnds 5 and 6, roughly 6 stitches apart. Begin to stuff.

Rnd 14: (1sc, dec) x6 [12]

Rnd 15: 6dec [6]

Fasten off and seal hole (see page 35 for instructions).

MUZZLE
In dark brown

Rnd 1: Ch 6 [6]

Rnd 2: Skip 2 stitches, 4hdc [4]

Fasten off and leave a long tail for sewing. Sew the muzzle directly between the two eyes. The top of the muzzle should be between rnds 4 and 5 of the body, and the bottom should be between rnds 6 and 7.

Using black yarn, embroider a nose directly in the middle of the muzzle (see page 31 for instructions).

EARS X2
In dark brown

Rnd 1: Ch 5 [5]

Rnd 2: Skip first stitch, 1slst, 1sc, 1hdc, 1dc [4]

Fasten off and leave a long tail for sewing. Sew each ear between rnds 3 and 4 of the body. They should be on each side of the head. The front of each ear should be 3 stitches away from the nearest eye.

(continued)

LEGS X2

In beige

Rnd 1: 6sc into mc [6]

Rnd 2: (1sc, inc) x3 [9]

Rnd 3: 9sc [9]

Rnd 4: (1sc, dec) x3 [6]

Stuff lightly. Fasten off and leave a long tail for sewing. Sew the bottom of a leg between rnds 12 and 13 of the body, and the top of the foot between rnds 11 and 12. Sew down the rest of the leg so it is secure. The leg should be in line with an eye. Repeat this for the second leg.

ARMS X2

In beige

Rnd 1: 6sc into mc [6]

Rnd 2-Rnd 3: 6sc [6]

Fasten off and leave a long tail for sewing. Sew the arms between rnds 7 and 8 of the body. They should be directly in line with each eye.

TAIL

In beige

Rnd 1: Ch 4 [4]

Rnd 2: Skip first stitch, 1slst, 1sc, 1hdc [3]

Fasten off and leave a long tail for sewing. Sew the tail between rnds 11 and 12 of the body. It should be directly in the middle of the back of the two ears.

PIG

And on the farm, there was a Pig! Next, we revisit some classic farm animals, starting with this quirky little piggy. This Pig project is an opportunity to practice sewing again, as there are a number of different parts you have to sew into place in order to achieve the adorable finished project.

MAIN BODY
Starting with the top of the head In light pink

Rnd 1: 6sc into mc [6]

Rnd 2: 6inc [12]

Rnd 3: (1sc, inc) x6 [18]

Rnd 4: (2sc, inc) x6 [24]

Rnd 5–Rnd 8: 24sc [24]

Rnd 9: (2sc, dec) x6 [18]

Rnd 10: (1sc, dec) x6 [12]

Place eyes between rnds 7 and 8, roughly 6 stitches apart. Do not embroider the mouth yet.

Begin to stuff.

Rnd 11: In FLO, (1sc, inc) x6 [18]

Rnd 12–Rnd 14: 18sc [18]

Rnd 15: (1sc, dec) x6 [12]

Make sure to continue stuffing.

Rnd 16: 6dec [6]

Fasten off and seal hole (see page 35 for instructions).

NOSE
In a different shade of pink than the body

Rnd 1: Ch 4 [4]

Rnd 2: Skip first stitch and turn, 3sc, now working on the other side of the ch (see page 38 for instructions), 3sc [6]

Fasten off and leave a long tail for sewing. Sew the nose directly between the two eyes. The top of the nose should roughly be between rnds 6 and 7, and the bottom of the nose should be between rnds 8 and 9. Sew down the rest of the nose so it is secure.

Using dark-brown yarn, embroider two nostrils on the nose with a running stitch. Below the nose, embroider a small mouth (see page 28 for instructions).

(continued)

PIG (CONTINUED)

EARS X2

In light pink

Rnd 1: Ch 6 [6]

Rnd 2: Skip first ch, slst, 1sc, 1hdc, 1dc, 1tr [5]

Fasten off and leave a long tail for sewing. Sew one end of the bottom of the ears between rnds 2 and 3 of the body, and the other end between rnds 5 and 6 of the body. Make sure that it is on each side of the head, roughly 3 to 4 stitches behind the eye. Sew down the rest of the ear, and repeat this step for the second ear.

ARMS AND LEGS X4

In light pink

Rnd 1: 6sc into mc [6]

Rnd 2–Rnd 3: 6sc [6]

Fasten off and leave a long tail for sewing.

For the arms: Fold each arm in half and sew the two sides together. Sew the arms between rnds 13 and 14 of the body, each arm directly beneath each eye.

For the legs: Sew the top of one leg between rnds 13 and 14 of the body, and the bottom between rnds 14 and 15. Sew down the rest of the leg. Make sure that it is next to the arm, with one stitch between them. Repeat this for the other leg.

TAIL

In light pink

Rnd 1: Ch 4 [4]

Rnd 2: Skip first stitch, (3sc all into the same stitch) x3 [9]

Fasten off and leave a long tail for sewing. Sew the tail between rnds 14 and 15. The tail should be directly between the two back legs.

COW

Back to more firm beginner favorites: the Cow! This Cow pattern allows you to stretch your ability when you practice the Joining Legs technique (page 41) needed for so many cute amigurumi. This is a really handy skill to have, and it is easy once you get the hang of it!

LEGS X2
Starting at the bottom of the hooves
In black

Rnd 1: 6sc into mc [6]

Rnd 2: 6sc [6]

Change color to white (see page 43 for instructions).

Rnd 3-Rnd 5: 6sc [6]

Fasten off the first leg.

Do not fasten off the second leg.

BODY
Carrying on from the legs

Carrying on from the second leg, we will now be joining the two legs together (see page 41 for instructions).

Rnd 6: Ch 1, sc into the side of the first leg, 5sc, 1sc into the back of the joining ch, 6sc into the second leg [14]

Rnd 7: 1sc into the front of the joining ch, 13sc [14]

Stuff the legs.

Rnd 8-Rnd 10: 14sc [14]

Rnd 11: (2sc, dec) x3, 2sc [11]

Rnd 12: In FLO, 11inc [22]

Stuff the body.

Rnd 13: 3sc, inc (the increases should be at the front and back of the head), 10sc, inc, 7sc [24]

Rnd 14-Rnd 17: 24sc [24]

Place eyes between rnds 15 and 16, roughly 4 to 5 stitches apart.

Rnd 18: (2sc, dec) x6 [18]

Begin to stuff the head.

Rnd 19: (1sc, dec) x6 [12]

Rnd 20: 6dec [6]

Fasten off and seal hole (see page 35 for instructions).

NOSE
In pink

Rnd 1: Ch 4 [4]

Rnd 2: Skip first stitch, 3sc, now working on the other side of the ch (see page 38 for instructions), 3sc [6]

Fasten off and leave a long tail for sewing. Sew the top of the nose between rnds 16 and 17 of the body, and the bottom of the nose between rnds 14 and 15. Make sure that you sew down the nose securely and that it is in the middle of the two eyes.

(continued)

COW (CONTINUED)

EARS X2

In white

Rnd 1: 6sc into mc [6]

Rnd 2: 6sc [6]

Fasten off and leave a long tail for sewing. Fold the circle in half, and sew one end together to create a teardrop shape. Sew the ears between rnds 18 and 19 of the body, roughly 2 stitches away from the closest eye.

HORNS X2

In beige

Rnd 1: 5sc into mc [5]

Rnd 2: 5sc [5]

Fasten off and leave a long tail for sewing. Sew one side of a horn between rnds 18 and 19 of the body, and the other side between rnds 19 and 20. Make sure that it is directly next to the ear and in line with an eye. Repeat for the other horn.

ARMS X2

In black

Rnd 1: 6sc into mc [6]

Rnd 2: 6sc [6]

Change color to white.

Rnd 3–Rnd 6: 6sc [6]

Fasten off and leave a long tail for sewing. Sew the arms between rnds 11 and 12, on each side of the body.

PATCHES X3 (OR NUMBER OF YOUR CHOICE)

In black

Rnd 1: 6sc into mc [6]

Fasten off and leave a long tail for sewing. Sew the spots randomly around the body into whatever position you desire.

TAIL WITH TASSEL

In white

Rnd 1: Ch 4 [4]

Fasten off and leave a long tail for sewing.

In black

(You now need to make a tassel to add to the 4 chains of the white tail). Cut 3 pieces of medium-length black yarn.
Thread one of the pieces of yarn through an embroidery needle. Push the needle through the starting knot at the very tip of the chain (the ch 4). Pull the black yarn through, so it is going through the starting knot of the chain. Repeat this once more, with the second piece of black yarn.

With the final piece of black yarn, tie a knot around the pieces that have been threaded through the chain, to create a tassel. You now have a small tassel attached to the tail. Trim the tassel to whatever length you desire.

Finally, sew the free end of the tail directly between the back of the legs, between rnds 7 and 8 of the body.

BUNNY

Finally, no amigurumi book is complete without a cute Bunny. This is once again a slightly bigger project. There aren't many difficult techniques in this pattern, but it will take a bit more time than some of the earlier patterns. And more good news? This charming Bunny loves hanging out with the Frog from the Garden section (page 86), too!

MAIN BODY
Starting with the top of the head
In white

Rnd 1: 6sc into mc [6]

Rnd 2: 6inc [12]

Rnd 3: (1sc, inc) x6 [18]

Rnd 4: (2sc, inc) x6 [24]

Rnd 5: (3sc, inc) x6 [30]

Rnd 6–Rnd 10: 30sc [30]

Rnd 11: (3sc, dec) x6 [24]

Place eyes between rnds 8 and 9, roughly 5 stitches apart. Embroider the nose between the two eyes, using pink yarn (see page 31 for instructions).

Rnd 12: (2sc, dec) x6 [18]

Stuff.

Rnd 13: In FLO, (2sc, inc) x6 [24]

Rnd 14–Rnd 17: 24sc [24]

Rnd 18: (2sc, dec) x6 [18]

Stuff.

Rnd 19: (1sc, dec) x6 [12]

Rnd 20: 6 dec [6]

Fasten off and seal hole (see page 35 for instructions).

EARS X2
In white

Rnd 1: 6sc into mc [6]

Rnd 2: (1sc, inc) x3 [9]

Rnd 3: (2sc, inc) x3 [12]

Rnd 4–Rnd 8: 12sc [12]

Rnd 9: (2sc, dec) x3 [9]

Fasten off and leave a long tail for sewing. Sew one side of the ear between rnds 1 and 2, and then sew the other end between rnds 5 and 6. Once you have sewn each end of the ear onto the head, go in and sew the middle part of the ear onto the head, so everything has been sewn down and won't come off. Repeat this for the other ear, but on the other side of the head. The ears should be on each side of the eyes.

(continued)

BUNNY (CONTINUED)

LEGS X2

In white

Rnd 1: 6sc into mc [6]

Rnd 2: 6inc [12]

Rnd 3–Rnd 4: 12sc [12]

Rnd 5: (2sc, dec) x3 [9]

Fasten off and leave a long tail for sewing. Stuff the foot lightly. Sew each foot at the base of the bunny, each one directly underneath an eye. The top of the foot should be sewn roughly between rnds 17 and 18, and the bottom of the foot should be sewn roughly between rnds 18 and 19. You may need to adjust this to suit your bunny and preference.

ARMS X2

In white

Rnd 1: 6sc into mc [6]

Rnd 2–Rnd 5: 6sc [6]

Fasten off and leave a long tail for sewing. Sew the top of the arms above each foot and roughly between rnds 12 and 13. Move the hand slightly forward, so it looks like it is resting on its belly. Sew into place. Make sure to do this for both hands.

TAIL

In white

Rnd 1: 6sc into mc [6]

Rnd 2: 6sc [6]

Fasten off and leave a long tail for sewing. Sew the tail on the back of the bunny, between the two feet, roughly between rnds 17 and 18.

WOODLAND Friends

We love nature! As we finish with our farm friends, we are off to explore the forests and woods. If you have been following the order of the projects in this book, you should be feeling a bit more confident now in your amigurumi skills. But even if that isn't so, fear not! Anyone can have a go at these projects, no matter your skill—so long as you give yourself time and patience, especially when it comes to assembling the bigger projects, such as the Fox (page 140)! And, as with all our sections, we throw in a couple of simpler and quicker patterns for ease and fun!

ACORN

In this section, we'll start you off gently with a fun little Acorn buddy. This little guy is a quick make—perfect as a little gift or as a sweet backpack charm for fall fun.

MAIN BODY
Starting at the bottom
In light brown

Rnd 1: 6sc into mc [6]

Rnd 2: (1sc, inc) x3 [9]

Rnd 3: (2sc, inc) x3 [12]

Rnd 4: (3sc, inc) x3 [15]

Rnd 5: (4sc, inc) x3 [18]

Rnd 6-Rnd 7: 18sc [18]

Rnd 8: (4sc, dec) x3 [15]

Place eyes between rnds 6 and 7, roughly 3 stitches apart. Sew one long running stitch between the two eyes to create the mouth.

Rnd 9: (3sc, dec) x3 [12]

Stuff.

Rnd 10: 6dec [6]

Fasten off and seal hole (see page 35 for instructions).

ACORN CAP
In dark brown

Rnd 1: 6sc into mc [6]

Rnd 2: 6inc [12]

Rnd 3: (1sc, inc) x6 [18]

Rnd 4: (5sc, inc) x3 [21]

Rnd 5-Rnd 6: 21sc [21]

Fasten off and leave a long tail for sewing. Place the cap onto the top of the acorn (where you made the final rnds), positioning it as desired. Sew the cap into place so it is secure.

ACORN STALK
In dark brown

Rnd 1: Ch 4 [4]

Rnd 2: Skip first stitch, 3sc [3]

Fasten off and leave a long tail for sewing. Sew one side of the stalk between rnds 1 and 2 of the cap, and sew the other side of the stalk on the other side of the mc made in the cap, between rnds 1 and 2. Make sure that the flat part of the stalk is facing the same side that the eyes and mouth are on.

PUMPKIN

Of course we needed to sneak a Pumpkin friend in for you. This quick project, which is basically another simple crochet ball, uses a clever sewing technique to add the segments.

PUMPKIN BODY

Starting at the top
In orange

Rnd 1: 6sc into mc [6]

Rnd 2: 6inc [12]

Rnd 3: (1sc, inc) x6 [18]

Rnd 4: (2sc, inc) x6 [24]

Rnd 5–Rnd 8: 24sc [24]

Rnd 9: (2sc, dec) x6 [18]

Place eyes between rnds 6 and 7, roughly 5 stitches apart. Don't embroider the mouth just yet. Begin to stuff.

Rnd 10: (1sc, dec) x6 [12]

Rnd 11: 6dec [6]

Fasten off and seal hole (see page 35 for instructions).

Using a long piece of yarn, insert an embroidery needle through the closing ring of your last rnd, and create a stitch that goes all the way over the body and into the starting mc. Pull the yarn tight, so you have made a large dent in the pumpkin. Repeat this 3 more times to create the ribs of the pumpkin. You may want to add more ribs, depending on your preference.

Embroider a mouth between the eyes (see page 28 for instructions).

STALK

In brown

Rnd 1: Ch 4 [4]

Rnd 2: Skip first stitch, 3sc [3]

Fasten off and leave a long tail for sewing. Sew one side of the stalk between rnds 1 and 2 of the pumpkin, and sew the other side of the stalk on the other side of the mc made in the pumpkin, between rnds 1 and 2. Make sure that the flat part of the stalk is facing the same side that the eyes and mouth are on.

MOUSE

Next, we add a little Mouse. The Mouse can be made in any color, and it works up really quickly. This pattern will help you practice creating different shapes and placing eyes into different positions. Not only would it be a great plushie for yourself, but also if you embroider on some eyes—and maybe add a little catnip—you will have yourself the perfect cat toy!

MOUSE BODY
Starting with the nose
In grey

Rnd 1: 6sc into mc [6]

Rnd 2: (1sc, inc) x3 [9]

Rnd 3: (2sc, inc) x3 [12]

Rnd 4: (3sc, inc) x3 [15]

Rnd 5: (4sc, inc) x3 [18]

Rnd 6: (5sc, inc) x3 [21]

Rnd 7–Rnd 11: 21sc [21]

Place eyes between rnds 5 and 6, roughly 5 stitches apart. Embroider a nose in pink, roughly between rnds 2 and 3 (see page 31 for instructions).

Rnd 12: (5sc, dec) x3 [18]

Stuff.

Rnd 13: (1sc, dec) x6 [12]

Rnd 14: 6dec [6]

Fasten off and seal hole (see page 35 for instructions).

EARS X2
In grey

Rnd 1: 7dc into mc [7]

Fasten off and leave a long tail for sewing. Sew the ears between rnds 7 and 8 of the body. They should be 3 stitches apart. Make sure that they are directly above the eyes.

TAIL
In grey

Rnd 1: Ch 12 [12]

Fasten off and leave a long tail for sewing. Sew the tail in the center of the closing ring.

LOAF REINDEER

Since the Loaf Cats (page 108) are so fun to make, we thought a Loaf Reindeer would be cute too. (This would also be a great winter project!) Once you have had a go at both the cat and the reindeer, perhaps you will even think of some of your own creations to try, like mixing and matching the Pug features (page 111) with the loaf body. We hope all of these projects will inspire you to start designing your own amigurumi minis!

MAIN PART OF THE HEAD
Starting with the face of the reindeer
In dark brown

Rnd 1: 6sc into mc [6]

Rnd 2: 6inc [12]

Rnd 3: (1sc, inc) x6 [18]

Rnd 4: (2sc, inc) x6 [24]

Rnd 5–Rnd 10: 24sc [24]

Place eyes between rnds 3 and 4, on each side of the mc (rnd 1).

Rnd 11: (2sc, dec) x6 [18]

Begin to stuff.

Rnd 12: (1sc, dec) x6 [12]

Rnd 13: 6dec [6]

Fasten off and seal hole (see page 35 for instructions).

MUZZLE
In light brown

Rnd 1: 6sc into mc [6]

Rnd 2: (1sc, inc) x3 [9]

Fasten off and leave a long tail for sewing. Sew the muzzle directly between the eyes. The mc of the muzzle (rnd 1) should be in line with the mc of the body.

Embroider a nose on the muzzle, making sure it is in line with the eyes (see page 31 for instructions).

ANTLERS X2
In light brown

Rnd 1: Ch 6 [6]

Rnd 2: Skip first stitch, 2slst, ch 3 – skip first stitch of the ch, 2slst down the ch – 3slst back into the original ch [7]

Fasten off and leave a long tail for sewing. Sew the antlers between rnds 5 and 6, placing each antler directly above an eye.

(continued)

The BIG BOOK of BEGINNER AMIGURUMI

EARS X2

In dark brown

Rnd 1: Ch 4 [4]

Rnd 2: Skip first stitch, 1sc, 1dc, 1sc [3]

Fasten off and leave a long tail for sewing. Sew each ear between rnds 5 and 6, directly next to the outside of each antler.

LEGS X4

In dark brown

Rnd 1: 7sc into mc [7]

Rnd 2–Rnd 3: 7sc [7]

Fasten off and leave a long tail for sewing. For the two front legs, sew the front of one of the legs between rnds 6 and 7 and the back of the leg between rnds 8 and 9.

Sew down the rest of the leg, and repeat the steps for the other front leg. Make sure that both legs are in line with the eyes.

For the two back legs, sew the front of one leg between rnds 10 and 11 and the back of the leg between rnds 12 and 13. Sew down the rest of the leg, and repeat the steps for the other back leg. Make sure that both legs are in line with the front legs.

TAIL

In dark brown

Rnd 1: Ch 4 [4]

Rnd 2: Skip first stitch, 3sc [3]

Fasten off and leave a long tail for sewing. Sew the tail between rnds 12 and 13, directly in line with the middle of the antlers.

SQUIRREL

Your Acorn (page 125) needs a Squirrel buddy to give it company, so let's make a cute little kawaii Squirrel. This adorable project would look even better using plush yarn!

MAIN BODY
Starting with the top of the head
In dark orange or red

Rnd 1: 6sc into mc [6]

Rnd 2: 6inc [12]

Rnd 3: (1sc, inc) x6 [18]

Rnd 4–Rnd 6: 18sc [18]

Change color to white (see page 43 for instructions).

Rnd 7: 18sc [18]

Rnd 8: (1sc, dec) x6 [12]

Change color to orange.

Rnd 9: In FLO, (1sc, inc) x6 [18]

Place eyes between rnds 6 and 7, roughly 5 stitches apart. Embroider a small nose between the eyes, using two running stitches (see page 31 for instructions).

Rnd 10–Rnd 11: 18sc [18]

Rnd 12: (1sc, dec) x6 [12]

Stuff.

Rnd 13: 6dec [6]

Fasten off and seal hole (see page 35 for instructions).

EARS X2
In orange

Rnd 1: Into a mc, 1sc, 1dc, 1sc [3]

Fasten off and leave a long tail for sewing. Sew one side of the ear between rnds 1 and 2 of the body, and the other side of the ear between rnds 3 and 4 of the body. (Repeat this for both ears.) Make sure they are in line with the eyes.

(continued)

SQUIRREL (CONTINUED)

ARMS X2

In orange

Rnd 1: 4sc into mc [4]

Rnd 2-Rnd 3: 4sc [4]

Fasten off and leave a long tail for sewing. Sew the top of the arm between rnds 8 and 9 of the body, and sew the bottom of the arm between rnds 9 and 10 of the body. Sew the rest of the arm into place, making sure it is facing inward toward the stomach. (Repeat this for both arms.)

LEGS X2

In orange

Rnd 1: 6sc into mc [6]

Rnd 2-Rnd 3: 6sc [6]

Fasten off and leave a long tail for sewing. Sew the bottom of the foot between rnds 11 and 12 of the body, and sew the top of the foot between rnds 10 and 11. Sew down the rest of the foot so it is secured. (Repeat this for both legs.) Make sure the legs are directly underneath the eyes and the arms.

TAIL

In orange

Rnd 1: 6sc into mc [6]

Rnd 2: (1sc, inc) x3 [9]

Rnd 3-Rnd 9: 9sc [9]

Fasten off and leave a long tail for sewing. Bend over the tip of the tail, very slightly, and sew it into place. On the bottom of the tail, sew one side between rnds 8 and 9 of the body, and sew the other side between rnds 11 and 12 of the body. Sew down the rest of the tail, so it is securely in place. Make sure that the tail is at an angle, so it can be seen from the front.

MUSHROOM

All forest fun HAS to include a "mushi"—your little forest friend! Beware: This little Mushroom may be small, but she is still ridiculously cute. Take your time when attaching the different body parts, as they are quite small. Then step back and be proud of your sewing skills!

MAIN BODY
Starting with the head
In white

Rnd 1: 6sc into mc [6]

Rnd 2: 6inc [12]

Rnd 3: (1sc, inc) x6 [18]

Rnd 4-Rnd 7: 18sc [18]

Rnd 8: (1sc, dec) x6 [12]

Rnd 9: In FLO, (1sc, inc) x6 [18]

Place eyes between rnds 5 and 6, roughly 3 stitches apart. Embroider mouth between the eyes (see page 28 for instructions).

Rnd 10-Rnd 12: 18sc [18]

Rnd 13: (1sc, dec) x6 [12]

Stuff.

Rnd 14: 6dec [6]

Fasten off and seal hole (see page 35 for instructions).

FEET/ARMS X4
In white

Rnd 1: 6sc into mc [6]

Rnd 2-Rnd 3: 6sc [6]

Fasten off and leave a long tail for sewing. Sew the feet directly in line with the eyes. The bottom of the foot should be sewn between rnds 12 and 13 of the body, and the top of the foot should be sewn between rnds 11 and 12. Repeat for both feet. The arms should also be in line with the eyes. The bottom of the arm should be between rnds 10 and 11 of the body, and the top of the arm should be between rnds 9 and 10. Repeat for both arms.

MUSHROOM CAP
In red

Rnd 1: 6sc into mc [6]

Rnd 2: 6inc [12]

Rnd 3: (1sc, inc) x6 [18]

Rnd 4: 18sc [18]

Rnd 5: In FLO, (1dc, dc inc) x9 [27]

Rnd 6: 27sc [27]

Fasten off and leave a long tail for sewing. Place the cap onto the head of the body into your desired position. Sew the cap into place, leaving a small gap open. Put a little bit of stuffing into this gap to give the cap a bit more volume. Sew up the small hole and any other missed gaps.

Using white yarn, sew stitches around the cap to give the mushroom cute spots.

BAT

It's time to explore other forest creatures with this cute Bat, which is also a great way to practice your different stitches as you make the wings! If you are a fan of Halloween crafts, then this bat should be added to your must-make list for that fun holiday, too!

MAIN BODY
Starting with the top of the head
In purple

Rnd 1: 6sc into mc [6]

Rnd 2: 6inc [12]

Rnd 3: (1sc, inc) x6 [18]

Rnd 4–Rnd 7: 18sc [18]

Rnd 8: (1sc, dec) x6 [12]

Place eyes between rnds 5 and 6, roughly 4 stitches apart. Embroider a mouth (see page 28 for instructions).

Rnd 9: In FLO, (1sc, inc) x6 [18]

Rnd 10–Rnd 12: 18sc [18]

Stuff.

Rnd 13: (1sc, dec) x6 [12]

Rnd 14: 6dec [6]

Fasten off and seal hole (see page 35 for instructions).

WINGS X2
In purple

Rnd 1: Ch 9 [9]

Rnd 2: Skip first stitch, 8sc [8]

Rnd 3: Ch 1 and turn, 8sc [8]

Rnd 4: Ch 2 and turn, 1dc, ch 2, 1slst, (ch 2, 1dc, ch 2, 1slst) x3 [8]

Fasten off and leave a long tail for sewing. Sew the wings next to each other, directly in the middle of the back. The top of the wing should be between rnds 7 and 8 of the body, and the bottom of the wing should be between rnds 13 and 14.

EARS X2
In purple

Rnd 1: Into a mc, 1hdc, 2dc, 1hdc [4]

Fasten off and leave a long tail for sewing. Sew one side of the ear between rnds 1 and 2 of the body, and the other side of the ear between rnds 4 and 5 of the body. (Repeat this for both ears.) Make sure they are in line with the eyes.

FEET X2
In purple

Rnd 1: 6sc into mc [6]

Fasten off and leave a long tail for sewing. Sew the feet between rnds 13 and 14. Make sure they are in line with the eyes.

FOX

MAIN BODY
Starting with the top of the head
In orange

Rnd 1: 6sc into mc [6]

Rnd 2: 6inc [12]

Rnd 3: (1sc, inc) x6 [18]

Rnd 4: (2sc, inc) x6 [24]

Rnd 5: (3sc, inc) x6 [30]

Rnd 6-Rnd 8: 30sc [30]

Change color to white (see page 43 for instructions).

Rnd 9-Rnd 10: 30sc [30]

Rnd 11: (3sc, dec) x6 [24]

Place eyes between rnds 8 and 9, roughly 5 stitches apart. Embroider the nose between the two eyes, using brown yarn (see page 31 for instructions).

Rnd 12: (2sc, dec) x6 [18]

Stuff. Change color to orange.

Rnd 13: In FLO, (2sc, inc) x6 [24]

Rnd 14-Rnd 17: 24sc [24]

Rnd 18: (2sc, dec) x6 [18]

Stuff.

Rnd 19: (1sc, dec) x6 [12]

Rnd 20: 6dec [6]

Fasten off and seal hole (see page 35 for instructions).

EARS X2
In black

Rnd 1: 6sc into mc [6]

Rnd 2: (1sc, inc) x3 [9]

Change color to orange.

Rnd 3: 9sc [9]

Rnd 4: (2sc, inc) x3 [12]

Rnd 5: 12sc [12]

Fasten off and leave a long tail for sewing. Sew one side of the ear between rnds 2 and 3 of the head, and sew the other side between rnds 6 and 7. Sew down the rest of the ear, so it is secure. Repeat this for both ears.

(continued)

FOX (CONTINUED)

LEGS X2

In orange

Rnd 1: 6sc into mc [6]

Rnd 2: 6inc [12]

Rnd 3-Rnd 4: 12sc [12]

Rnd 5: (2sc, dec) x3 [9]

Fasten off and leave a long tail for sewing. Stuff the foot lightly. Sew each foot at the base of the fox. Each foot should be slightly to the side of an eye. The top of the foot should be sewn roughly between rnds 17 and 18, and the bottom of the foot should be sewn roughly between rnds 18 and 19. You may need to adjust this to suit your fox and your personal preference.

ARMS X2

In black

Rnd 1: 6sc into mc [6]

Rnd 2: 6sc [6]

Change color to orange.

Rnd 3-Rnd 5: 6sc [6]

Fasten off and leave a long tail for sewing. Sew the top of the arms next to each foot, roughly between rnds 13 and 14. Make sure each arm is directly beneath an eye. Sew a stitch or two at the back of the arms to attach them to the fox's stomach.

TAIL

In white

Rnd 1: 6sc into mc [6]

Rnd 2: 6sc [6]

Change color to orange.

Rnd 3: (1sc, inc) x3 [9]

Rnd 4: 9sc [9]

Rnd 5: (2sc, inc) x3 [12]

Rnd 6: (1sc, inc) x6 [18]

Rnd 7-Rnd 8: 18sc [18]

Rnd 9: (1sc, dec) x6 [12]

Rnd 10: 12sc [12]

Rnd 11: (2sc, dec) x3 [9]

Rnd 12: 9sc [9]

Fasten off and leave a long tail for sewing. Stuff lightly—don't put much in. Sew the tail between the back legs. The tail should be at an angle, so it can be seen from the front. One side of the tail should be between rnds 12 and 13 of the body. The other side of the tail should roughly be between rnds 16 and 17.

Frosty FUN

Brrrr! This part of the book is quite cold! Once again, you will find a fantastic mix of projects at different skill levels to enjoy. From the Snowman (page 147) to the Walrus (page 157), these frosty cuties make great ornaments, gifts, and decorations for the winter holidays—as well as lovely plushies using different types of yarn.

SNOWMAN

Let's start off quick and easy with a little Snowman: a perfect keychain or holiday ornament. The scarf is a great opportunity to use up some of your colorful yarn scraps. When you're creating that tiny little carrot nose, make sure to keep your stitches quite tight so you don't end up with a massive nose that is out of proportion with the face. Also, recognize that creating the tiny nose may be a little fiddly, so don't worry if you don't get it on your first try; just have another go!

MAIN BODY
Starting with the top of the head
In white

Rnd 1: 6sc into mc [6]

Rnd 2: 6inc [12]

Rnd 3: (1sc, inc) x6 [18]

Rnd 4-Rnd 6: 18sc [18]

Rnd 7: (1sc, dec) x6 [12]

Rnd 8: In FLO, (1sc, inc) x6 [18]

Place eyes between rnds 4 and 5, roughly 5 stitches apart.

Rnd 9: (2sc, inc) x6 [24]

Rnd 10-Rnd 11: 24sc [24]

Begin to stuff.

Rnd 12: (2sc, dec) x6 [18]

Rnd 13: (1sc, dec) x6 [12]

Rnd 14: 6dec [6]

Fasten off and seal hole (see page 35 for instructions).

BUTTONS

Using a long piece of black yarn, embroider 2 or 3 running stitches in the same spot between rnds 9 and 10, directly in line with the middle of the eyes.

Embroider another button between rnds 11 and 12, directly underneath the first button.

NOSE
In orange

Rnd 1: 4sc into mc [4]

Rnd 2: 4sc [4]

Fasten off and leave a long tail for sewing. Sew the nose directly between the eyes (see page 31 for instructions). The top of the nose should be sewn roughly between rnds 3 and 4, and the bottom of the nose should be sewn roughly between rnds 5 and 6.

(continued)

SNOWMAN (CONTINUED)

SCARF

In red

Rnd 1: Ch 40 [40]

Rnd 2: Skip first stitch, 39sc [39]

Fasten off and weave in ends. Tie the scarf around the neck of the snowman into whatever position you desire.

Optional: Using a long piece of red yarn, you can sew the scarf into place.

HAT

In black

Rnd 1: 6sc into mc [6]

Rnd 2: (1sc, inc) x3 [9]

Rnd 3: In BLO, 9sc [9]

Rnd 4–Rnd 5: 9sc [9]

Rnd 6: In FLO, 9inc [18]

Fasten off and weave in the ends.

Tie a long piece of red yarn around the hat, to create a ribbon. Trim away any unwanted long ends.

Feel free to place the hat into a position of your choice. You can decide whether to sew the hat into place or allow it to remain removable!

POLAR BEAR

Next, we have a gorgeous Polar Bear. This Polar Bear pattern is easy to make—though you will be practicing your skill of Joining Legs (page 41) to create a little amigurumi figure. And the scarf, again, gives you a chance to use up smaller yarn leftovers. This pattern upscales wonderfully in plush yarn, too!

LEGS X2
Starting at the bottom of the leg
In white

Rnd 1: 6sc into mc [6]

Rnd 2: 6sc [6]

Rnd 3: (1sc, inc) x3 [9]

Fasten off the first leg. Do not fasten off the second leg.

BODY
Carrying on from the legs

Carrying on from the second leg, we will now be joining the two legs (see page 41 for instructions).

Rnd 4: Ch 1, sc into the side of the first leg, 8sc in the rest of the first leg, 1sc into the back of the ch, 9sc into the second leg [20]

Rnd 5: 1sc into the front of the ch, 19sc [20]

Rnd 6-Rnd 8: 20sc [20]

Rnd 9: 4sc, dec (the dec should be on the side of the polar bear, so you may need to change this to fit your bear), 8sc, dec (the dec should be on the side of the bear again), 4sc [18]

Rnd 10: 3sc, dec (the dec should be on the side of the bear), 7sc, dec (the dec should be on the side of the bear), 4sc [16]

Start stuffing the body.

Rnd 11-Rnd 14: 16sc [16]

Place eyes between rnds 12 and 13, roughly 4 stitches apart.

Rnd 15: (2sc, dec) x4 [12]

Rnd 16: 6dec [6]

Fasten off and seal hole (see page 35 for instructions).

(continued)

POLAR BEAR (CONTINUED)

ARMS X2

In white

Rnd 1: 6sc into mc [6]

Rnd 2–Rnd 5: 6sc [6]

Fasten off and leave a long tail for sewing. Sew the arms between rnds 10 and 11. Make sure that they are sewn on each side of the body.

MUZZLE

In grey

Rnd 1: Ch 4 [4]

Rnd 2: Skip first stitch, 3sc [3]

Fasten off and leave a long tail for sewing. Sew the muzzle between the eyes. The top of the muzzle should be sewn between rnds 13 and 14, and the bottom of the muzzle should be sewn between rnds 11 and 12. Embroider a nose in the middle of the muzzle, using brown yarn (see page 31 for instructions).

EARS X2

In white

Rnd 1: 4sc into mc [4]

Fasten off and leave a long tail for sewing. Sew one side of the ear between rnd 16 and the closing ring of the body, and sew the other side of the ear between rnds 14 and 15. (Repeat this for the other ear.) Make sure that both ears are in line with the eyes.

SCARF

In scarf color of choice (e.g., light blue)

Rnd 1: Ch 35 [35]

Rnd 2: Skip 2 stitches, 33hdc [33]

Fasten off and leave a long tail for sewing. Wrap the scarf around the neck of the polar bear, and sew it into your chosen position.

SNOWY OWL

Snowy Owls are a great winter craft, and we love the shape of this one. You can switch out the colors and use it for other seasons, too. You will also be putting your sewing and embroidery skills to the test when you create those adorable feathers and the little pointy beak!

OWL BODY
Starting with the top of the head
In white

Rnd 1: 6sc into mc [6]

Rnd 2: 6inc [12]

Rnd 3: (1sc, inc) x6 [18]

Rnd 4: (2sc, inc) x6 [24]

Rnd 5–Rnd 7: 24sc [24]

Rnd 8: 7sc, 4inc, 13sc [28]

Rnd 9: 10sc, 2inc, 16sc [30]

Rnd 10–Rnd 12: 30sc [30]

Place eyes between rnds 5 and 6, roughly 5 stitches apart. The eyes should be on the other side of the spot where the increases in rnds 8 and 9 have been made (the increases are placed at the back of the owl to form the tail). Embroider a pointy beak between the two eyes (see page 30 for instructions).

Rnd 13: (3sc, dec) x6 [24]

Begin to stuff.

Rnd 14: (2sc, dec) x6 [18]

Rnd 15: (1sc, dec) x6 [12]

Rnd 16: 6dec [6]

Fasten off and seal hole (see page 35 for instructions).

WINGS X2
In grey

Rnd 1: 6dc into a mc [6]

Rnd 2: Ch 2 and turn, 6hdc [6]

Rnd 3: Ch 1 and turn, 6sc [6]

Fasten off and leave a long tail for sewing. The beginning rnd of the wing, where the 6dc was made, should be facing toward the tail of the owl. Sew the top of the wing between rnds 6 and 7 of the body, and sew the bottom of the wing between rnds 13 and 14. Sew down the rest of the wing. Repeat this for both wings, making sure that they are placed on each side of the body.

Using grey yarn, sew V-shaped stitches between the two wings to create the feathers of the owl. Create the V shape by sewing two diagonal running stitches between two rnds of the body.

SEAL

If you have a set of frosty friends, you will of course also need a baby Seal. This one is super-quick and easy to make! Just be sure to take your time over the tail flippers, and follow the instructions closely.

SEAL BODY
Starting with the face
In white

Rnd 1: 6sc into mc [6]

Rnd 2: 6inc [12]

Rnd 3: (1sc, inc) x6 [18]

Rnd 4–Rnd 8: 18sc [18]

Place one eye between rnds 2 and 3 and the other eye between rnds 3 and 4, on each side of the mc (roughly 5 stitches apart). The eyes have been placed in this position so they aren't as close together, but depending on your crochet, you may need to change the positions of each eye in order for it to look how you would like it to.

Begin to stuff.

Rnd 9: (4sc, dec) x3 [15]

Rnd 10: (3sc, dec) x3 [12]

Rnd 11: (2sc, dec) x3 [9]

Rnd 12: (1sc, dec) x3 [6]

Fasten off and seal hole (see page 35 for instructions).

MUZZLE
In grey

Rnd 1: Into a mc, 1sc, 1dc, 1slst, 1dc, 1sc [5]

Fasten off and leave a long tail for sewing. Sew the muzzle directly between the two eyes, making sure that it isn't too low on the face or too high. Using brown yarn, embroider a nose onto the muzzle (see page 31 for instructions). Make sure that the top of the nose is in line with the top of the muzzle; you don't want it to be too low or too high.

SIDE FLIPPERS X2
In white

Rnd 1: 5sc into mc [5]

Fasten off and leave a long tail for sewing. Sew one side of a flipper between rnds 6 and 7 and the other side between rnds 8 and 9 of the body. Make sure that the flipper is in line with the closest eye. Repeat this for the other flipper.

TAIL FLIPPERS X2
In white

Rnd 1: Ch 5 [5]

Rnd 2: Skip 2 stitches, 1dc, 1hdc, 1sc [3]

Fasten off and leave a long tail for sewing. Sew the flippers between rnd 12 and the closing ring of the body. The flippers should be sewn directly next to each other, side by side. Make sure that the "neat" side of the crochet is facing upward.

WALRUS

Let's make a chonky, happy Walrus to keep the Seal (page 154) company! As with the nose of the Snowman (page 147), the teeth are quite small. Take your time making them, and take extra care when you are sewing them in place.

WALRUS BODY
Starting with the top of the head
In brown

Rnd 1: 6sc into mc [6]

Rnd 2: 6inc [12]

Rnd 3: (1sc, inc) x6 [18]

Rnd 4–Rnd 6: 18sc [18]

Rnd 7: 3sc, 5hdc inc, 6sc, inc, 3sc [24]

Rnd 8: 7sc, 2inc, 15sc [26]

Rnd 9: 7sc, 4inc, 15sc [30]

Rnd 10: 30sc [30]

Place eyes between rnds 4 and 5, 4 stitches apart. Make sure that the spot where the hdcs were made in rnd 7 are on the other side of the eyes (because rnd 7 is the start of the tail).

Rnd 11: (3sc, dec) x6 [24]

Rnd 12: (2sc, dec) x6 [18]

Stuff.

Rnd 13: (1sc, dec) x6 [12]

Rnd 14: 6dec [6]

Fasten off and seal hole (see page 35 for instructions).

MUZZLE X2
In beige

Rnd 1: 5sc into mc [5]

Fasten off and leave a long tail for sewing. Make sure that the hole in the circle is pulled tight. Sew the two circles together to create an 8 shape. Sew the top of the muzzle between rnds 4 and 5 of the body, and sew the bottom of the muzzle between rnds 6 and 7. Make sure that it is directly between the eyes. Leave the bottom of the muzzle open (don't sew it down).

TEETH X2
In white

Rnd 1: Ch 4 [4]

Rnd 2: Skip first stitch, slst, 2sc [3]

Fasten off and leave a long tail for sewing. Tuck one tooth on each side of the part of the muzzle that had not been sewn down. Sew down the teeth. Sew down the rest of the muzzle.

Sew on a T nose at the top of the muzzle (see page 31 for instructions).

(continued)

WALRUS (CONTINUED)

TAIL X2

In brown

Rnd 1: Ch 7 [7]

Rnd 2: Skip 2 stitches, 2 dc, 1hdc, 1sc, 1slst [5]

Fasten off and leave a long tail for sewing. Sew the two separate tail pieces directly next to each other between rnds 10 and 11 of the body. They should be on the opposite side of the eyes.

FLIPPERS X2

In brown

Rnd 1: Ch 9 [9]

Rnd 2: Skip 2 stitches, 5dc, 2hdc [7]

Fasten off and leave a long tail for sewing. Sew the top of each flipper between rnds 6 and 7 of the body. Sew down the rest of the flipper—but not all the way. Make sure that the bottom is left loose so it can flip up. Each flipper should be 1 stitch away from the outside of the nearest eye.

CARDINAL

CARDINAL BODY
Starting with the top of the head
In red

Rnd 1: 6sc into mc [6]

Rnd 2: 6inc [12]

Rnd 3: (1sc, inc) x6 [18]

Rnd 4: 7sc, change color to black (see page 43 for instructions), 4sc, change color to red, 7sc [18]

Rnd 5: 7sc, change color to black, 5sc, change color to red, 6sc [18]

Rnd 6: 8sc, change color to black, 3sc, change color to red, 7sc [18]

Rnd 7: 2inc, 6sc, 3inc, 6sc, inc [24]

Rnd 8: 3hdc inc, 21sc [27]

Place eyes between rnds 4 and 5, roughly 3 to 4 stitches apart. The eyes should be positioned at each end of the black face markings.

Rnd 9-Rnd 10: 27sc [27]

Rnd 11: (2sc, dec) x6, 3sc [21]

Rnd 12: (1sc, dec) x7 [14]

Begin to stuff.

Rnd 13: 7dec [7]

Fasten off and seal hole (see page 35 for instructions).

WINGS X2
In red

Rnd 1: Into a mc, 1sc, 1hdc, 2dc, 1hdc, 1sc [6]

Do not join the stitches to form a circle, because you want the wing to have a flat side.

Fasten off and leave a long tail for sewing. Sew each wing between rnds 7 and 8 of the body, placing one on each side of the body. Make sure the front of each wing is in line with the corresponding eye.

(continued)

FEATHER TUFTS X2

In red

Rnd 1: Ch 4 [4]

Rnd 2: Skip first stitch, 3slst [3]

Fasten off and leave a long tail for sewing. Sew one of the tufts between rnds 1 and 2 of the body, making sure that the neat, flat side is facing forward. Also make sure that it is on the side closest to the face. Sew the second tuft also between rnds 1 and 2, but make sure it is on the opposite side of the mc (first rnd of the body) to the first tuft. Sew it at a slight angle, so it peeks out from behind the first tuft.

BEAK

In orange

Rnd 1: 3sc into mc [3]

Rnd 2: 3sc [3]

Fasten off and leave a long tail for sewing. Sew the beak directly between the eyes. The top of the beak should be between rnds 4 and 5 of the body, and the bottom of the beak should be sewn roughly between rnds 5 and 6. Sew down the rest of the beak, and make sure that it is secure.

FEET X2

In orange

Rnd 1: Ch 4 [4]

Rnd 2: Skip first stitch, 1sc, 1hdc, 1sc [3]

Fasten off and leave a long tail for sewing. Sew the feet between rnds 11 and 12 of the body. Make sure that each foot lines up with each eye.

GINGERBREAD MAN

Finally, a small project that gives you practice working on tiny amigurumi: the Gingerbread Man! This little guy is fiddly—especially those tiny buttons and legs! But it's all truly worth it, because he is oh-so-fun to make!

LEGS X2
Starting at the bottom of the leg
In brown

Rnd 1: 6sc into mc [6]

Rnd 2–Rnd 3: 6sc [6]

Fasten off first leg and weave in ends. Do not fasten off the second leg.

BODY
Carrying on from the legs

Carrying on from the second leg, we will now be joining the two legs (see page 41 for instructions).

Rnd 4: 1sc into the side of the first leg, 5sc, 1sc back into the second leg, 5sc [12]

Rnd 5–Rnd 6: 12sc [12]

Rnd 7: (1sc, dec) x4 [8]

Begin to stuff.

HEAD
Continuing from the body

Rnd 8: 8inc [16]

Rnd 9–Rnd 11: 16sc [16]

Rnd 12: (2sc, dec) x4 [12]

Place eyes between rnds 9 and 10, roughly 3 stitches apart. Embroider a mouth between the eyes, using white yarn (see page 28 for instructions).

Stuff.

Rnd 13: 6dec [6]

Fasten off and seal hole (see page 35 for instructions).

ARMS X2
In brown

Rnd 1: 5sc into mc [5]

Rnd 2–Rnd 3: 5sc [5]

Fasten off and leave a long tail for sewing. Sew the top of each arm between rnds 7 and 8, on each side of the eyes. Sew down the rest of the arm to make sure everything is securely in place.

(continued)

BUTTONS X2

In red

Rnd 1: 3sc into mc [3]

Change color to white (see page 43 for instructions).

Rnd 2: 3sc, 1slst into the first stitch of the rnd [3]

Fasten off and leave a long tail for sewing. Sew the top of one of the buttons between rnds 7 and 8, and sew the bottom of that button between rnds 6 and 7. Make sure that the button is directly in line with the mouth. Sew the top of the other button between rnds 5 and 6, and sew the bottom of that button between rnds 4 and 5. Make sure that it is directly in line with the other button.

FROSTING (ON THE ARMS AND LEGS)

Using white yarn, thread the needle between rnds 1 and 2 of the arm. Create a running stitch that goes all the way around the arm and back through the same hole it was threaded through in the first place. Repeat this for both arms and legs.

IN the ZOO

Be careful as you make your way through this section. There are so many irresistible creatures hiding along your journey, you may be unable to stop making them!

Since we are getting toward the end of the book, the patterns have gotten just a little bit more intricate. Now you can experience the wonders of slightly longer projects, lots of details, and a little more sewing. By now, you should feel much more confident in your crochet and sewing skills! Don't be intimidated—you've got this! Take on the challenge, and explore the wonders of this fun section!

MONKEY

This adorable Monkey is a must-make! The Monkey is a great project for continuing to practice those color changes. This technique will help you create an adorable cheeky face, so it is totally worth practicing this skill! The Monkey pattern also challenges you to create a whole new stitch: the 3 stitches together decrease. You can even consider adding a little VELCRO® or snap fasteners to the monkey's hands and feet for the perfect clinging toy you can enjoy anywhere!

HEAD
Starting at the top of the head
In brown

Rnd 1: 6sc into mc [6]

Rnd 2: 6inc [12]

Rnd 3: (1sc, inc) x6 [18]

Rnd 4: 18sc [18]

Now we are beginning to make the beige face, so we will be doing some color changes from brown to beige and back again (see page 43 for instructions).

Rnd 5: 6sc, change color to beige, 2sc, change color to brown, 1sc, change color to beige, 3sc, change color to brown, 6sc [18]

Rnd 6: 6sc, change color to beige, 7sc, change color to brown, 5sc [18]

Rnd 7: 6sc, change color to beige, 7sc, change color to brown, 5sc [18]

Rnd 8: 6sc, change color to beige, 7sc, change color to brown, 5sc [18]

Rnd 9: 7sc, change color to beige, 6sc, change color to brown, 5sc [18]

Insert safety eyes between rnds 6 and 7, roughly 4 stitches apart. Embroider a nose between the two eyes (see page 31 for instructions). Make the vertical stitch go down by two rows, rather than one row.

Rnd 10: (1sc, dec) x6 [12]

Stuff the head.

Rnd 11: 6dec [6]

Fasten off and seal hole (see page 35 for instructions).

EARS X2
In brown

Rnd 1: 5sc into mc [5]

Fasten off and leave a long tail. Sew one side of an ear between rnds 6 and 7 of the head, and sew the other side of the ear between rnds 8 and 9. The ear should be 2 or 3 stitches away from its closest eye. Repeat for the other ear.

(continued)

MONKEY (CONTINUED)

BODY

Starting at the bottom of the body
In brown

Rnd 1: 6sc [6]

Rnd 2: 6inc [12]

Rnd 3: (1sc, inc) x6 [18]

Rnd 4–Rnd 5: 18sc [18]

Rnd 6: 7sc, 3tog, 8sc [16]

Rnd 7: 16sc [16]

Rnd 8: 7sc, 3tog, 6sc [14]

Rnd 9: 14sc [14]

Rnd 10: (1sc, dec) x4, 2sc [10]

Stuff the body.

Fasten off and sew the monkey's body to the bottom of the monkey's head.

LEGS/ARMS X4

In brown

Rnd 1: Ch 27 [27]

Rnd 2: Skip 2 stitches, 25hdc [25]

Fasten off and leave a long tail for sewing.

For the arms: Sew each arm between rnds 9 and 10 of the body, roughly 4 to 5 stitches apart from each other. The arms should be in line with the eyes.

For the legs: Sew each leg between rnds 3 and 4 of the body, roughly 3 stitches apart from each other. The legs should be in line with the eyes.

AXOLOTL

Let's make a worldwide favorite: an Axolotl. This Axolotl is perfect in any color with any yarn! There are so many adorable color combinations that you can create—wouldn't it look cute in some purples or blues?

MAIN BODY
Starting with the top of the head
In light pink

Rnd 1: 6sc into mc [6]

Rnd 2: 6inc [12]

Rnd 3: (1sc, inc) x6 [18]

Rnd 4: (2sc, inc) x6 [24]

Rnd 5–Rnd 8: 24sc [24]

Rnd 9: (2sc, dec) x6 [18]

Rnd 10: (1sc, dec) x6 [12]

Place eyes between rnds 6 and 7, roughly 5 to 6 stitches apart. Embroider a mouth between the eyes, using brown or black yarn (see page 28 for instructions).

Begin to stuff.

Rnd 11: In FLO, (1sc, inc) x6 [18]

Rnd 12–Rnd 14: 18sc [18]

Rnd 15: (1sc, dec) x6 [12]

Make sure to continue stuffing.

Rnd 16: 6dec [6]

Now we are forming the tail.

Rnd 17–Rnd 19: 6sc [6]

Fasten off and seal hole (see page 35 for instructions).

TAIL FINS X2
In dark pink

Rnd 1: Ch 5 [5]

Rnd 2: Skip 2 stitches, 1hdc, 1slst, 1hdc [3]

Fasten off and leave a long tail for sewing. Sew one end of a tail fin between rnds 17 and 18 of the body. Sew the other end of the tail fin in the center of the closing circle that you should have formed when fastening off the body (rnd 19). Sew down the rest of the fin to make sure it is secure. Repeat for the other fin, making sure that each fin is on a different side of the body.

(continued)

GILLS X2
In dark pink

Rnd 1: Ch 8 [8]

Rnd 2: Skip 2 stitches, 1dc, slst, (ch 2, 1dc, slst) x2 [6]

Fasten off and leave a long tail for sewing. Sew one side of a gill between rnds 2 and 3 of the body, and sew the other side between rnds 7 and 8. Sew down the rest of the gill to make sure that it is secure. Repeat this for the second gill. Make sure that each gill is on one side of the head. Each gill should also be roughly 3 stitches away from the nearest eye.

FEET X2
In light pink

Rnd 1: 6sc into mc [6]

Rnd 2: (1sc, inc) x3 [9]

Rnd 3: 9sc [9]

Fasten off and leave a long tail for sewing. Sew the bottom of a foot between rnds 15 and 16 of the body. Sew the top of the foot between rnds 13 and 14 of the body. Sew down the rest of the foot to make sure it is secured. The foot should be in line with one of the eyes. Repeat this for the other foot.

ARMS X2
In light pink

Rnd 1: 6sc into mc [6]

Rnd 2–Rnd 4: 6sc [6]

Fasten off and leave a long tail for sewing. Sew one end of an arm between rnds 10 and 11 of the body, and sew the other side at a slight diagonal between rnds 12 and 13. Move the arm forward, so it appears to be resting on its stomach. Sew the arm into place. Repeat this for the other arm.

KOALA

We really love this little Koala because of his charming face. This pattern requires you to crochet together two sides, but by now you should find this to be really easy! (And don't worry if that's not the case—just keep practicing!)

MAIN BODY
Starting with the top of the head
In grey

Rnd 1: 6sc into mc [6]

Rnd 2: 6inc [12]

Rnd 3: (1sc, inc) x6 [18]

Rnd 4: (2sc, inc) x6 [24]

Rnd 5-Rnd 8: 24sc [24]

Rnd 9: (2sc, dec) x6 [18]

Rnd 10: In FLO, (2sc, inc) x6 [24]

Place eyes between rnds 6 and 7, 5 stitches apart.

Rnd 11-Rnd 13: 24sc [24]

Rnd 14: (2sc, dec) x6 [18]

Stuff.

Rnd 15: (1sc, dec) x6 [12]

Rnd 16: 6dec [6]

Fasten off and seal hole (see page 35 for instructions).

FEET X2
In grey

Rnd 1: 6sc into mc [6]

Rnd 2: 6inc [12]

Rnd 3-Rnd 4: 12sc [12]

Fasten off and leave a long tail for sewing. Sew the bottom of one of the feet between rnds 15 and 16 of the body, and the top between rnds 11 and 12. Lightly stuff the foot, and sew the rest of it down, so it is securely in place. Make sure that it is directly in line with one of the eyes. Repeat for the other foot.

ARMS X2
In grey

Rnd 1: 6sc into mc [6]

Rnd 2-Rnd 5: 6sc [6]

Fasten off and leave a long tail for sewing. Sew the top side of one of the arms between rnds 8 and 9 of the body, and the bottom side between rnds 11 and 12 (we are sewing the arm horizontally). Sew down the rest of the arm, and make sure that the arm appears to be resting on the koala's stomach. Repeat for the other arm. Each arm should line up with each eye.

(continued)

KOALA (CONTINUED)

EARS X2

In white

Rnd 1: 6sc into mc [6]

Rnd 2: 6inc [12]

Change color to grey (see page 43 for instructions).

Rnd 3: 12sc [12]

Rnd 4: Fold the ear in half, and crochet together the two sides (see page 36 for instructions), 6sc across [6]

Fasten off and leave a long tail for sewing. Sew the top end of one ear between rnds 2 and 3 of the body, and the bottom end of the ear between rnds 7 and 8. Make sure that the white part of the ear is in the inside, against the head. Sew down the rest of the ear to make sure it is securely in place. The ear should be 3 stitches away from the nearest eye. Repeat for the second ear.

NOSE

In black

Rnd 1: Ch 3 [3]

Rnd 2: Skip first stitch, 2sc [2]

Fasten off and leave a long tail for sewing. Sew the nose directly between the eyes. The top of the nose should be between rnds 5 and 6 of the body, and the bottom of the nose should be between rnds 7 and 8. Sew down the rest of the nose to ensure it is secure.

SLOTH

Who doesn't love a Sloth!? This cutie provides a little more challenge when making the detailed face, but don't worry. Approach this pattern one step at a time, and the results will be totally worth it! This pattern will put your sewing skills to the test—but overall, we think you will really enjoy creating this amigurumi!

MAIN BODY
Starting with the top of the head
In light brown

Rnd 1: 6sc into mc [6]

Rnd 2: 6inc [12]

Rnd 3: (1sc, inc) x6 [18]

Rnd 4: (2sc, inc) x6 [24]

Rnd 5–Rnd 10: 24sc [24]

Rnd 11: (2sc, dec) x6 [18]

Begin to stuff.

Rnd 12: (1sc, dec) x6 [12]

Rnd 13: 6dec [6]

Fasten off and seal hole (see page 35 for instructions).

FACE
In beige

Rnd 1: Ch 8 [8]

Rnd 2: Skip first stitch, 7sc, now working on the other side of the ch (see page 38 for instructions), 7sc [14]

Rnd 3: 14sc [14]

Fasten off and leave a long tail for sewing. Don't sew the face to the body yet.

EYE PATCHES X2
In dark brown

Rnd 1: Ch 4 [4]

Rnd 2: Skip first stitch, 3sc [3]

Fasten off and leave a long tail for sewing. Place the eye patches onto the face, so the more rounded edge is facing inward. Sew the other end of the patch in line with the side of the face. Make sure that the eye patches are pointing inward at a slight angle. Sew the patches into place once you are happy with the positioning.

(continued)

SLOTH (CONTINUED)

When you have securely sewn on the eye patches, place the eyes toward the inward end of each eye patch. Embroider a small nose using black yarn, directly between the gap of the two eye patches, by creating 2 running stitches on top of each other. Embroider a mouth a row below the nose so there is a 1-stitch gap between the bottom of the nose and the top of the mouth (see page 28 for instructions).

Once you are happy with the face, sew the top of the face between rnds 3 and 4 of the body, and the bottom of the face between rnds 7 and 8. Sew down the rest of the face so it is secure.

LEGS X2
In light brown

Rnd 1: 6sc into mc [6]

Rnd 2: (1sc, inc) x3 [9]

Rnd 3: 9sc [9]

Rnd 4: (1sc, dec) x3 [6]

Lightly stuff the foot.

Fasten off and leave a long tail for sewing. Sew the bottom of a foot between rnds 11 and 12 of the body, and the top of the foot between rnds 10 and 11. Sew down the rest of the foot so it is secure. Make sure that it is directly below one of the eyes. Repeat this for the other foot.

ARMS X2
In light brown

Rnd 1: 6sc into mc [6]

Rnd 2–Rnd 6: 6sc [6]

Fasten off and leave a long tail for sewing. Sew arms between rnds 6 and 7, on each side of the body. Each arm should be roughly 1 stitch away from the face.

GIRAFFE

This joyful, bright-yellow Giraffe definitely adds a splash of color to this section! Although this charming project does not require many complicated stitches, it does put your sewing skills to the test as you attach all of those adorable little features.

HEAD
Starting with the nose
In beige

Rnd 1: 6sc into mc [6]

Rnd 2: 6inc [12]

Rnd 3-Rnd 4: 12sc [12]

Change color to yellow (see page 43 for instructions).

Rnd 5: 4sc, inc, 2hdc inc, inc, 4sc [16]

Rnd 6: 7sc, 2inc, 7sc [18]

Rnd 7-Rnd 8: 18sc [18]

Place eyes between rnds 5 and 6, roughly 4 stitches apart. Make sure that the rnd with the 2hdc inc (rnd 5) is the forehead of your giraffe.

Begin to stuff.

Rnd 9: (1sc, dec) x6 [12]

Rnd 10: 6dec [6]

Fasten off and seal hole (see page 35 for instructions).

BODY
Starting from the bottom
In yellow

Rnd 1: 6sc into mc [6]

Rnd 2: 6inc [12]

Rnd 3: (1sc, inc) x6 [18]

Rnd 4-Rnd 8: 18sc [18]

Rnd 9: (1sc, dec) x6 [12]

Begin to stuff.

Rnd 10: 6dec [6]

Rnd 11-Rnd 13: 6sc [6]

Fasten off and leave a long tail for sewing. Fold the top of the neck in half, and sew along the edge. Sew the neck between rnds 9 and 10 of the head. Make sure that it is securely in place.

LEGS X2
In brown

Rnd 1: 8sc into mc [8]

Rnd 2: 8sc [8]

Change color to yellow.

Rnd 3-Rnd 6: 8sc [8]

Fasten off and leave a long tail for sewing. Sew each leg between rnds 3 and 4 of the body. They should be roughly 5 stitches apart. Make sure that they are in line with the eyes.

(continued)

GIRAFFE (CONTINUED)

ARMS X2

In brown

Rnd 1: 7sc into mc [7]

Rnd 2: 7sc [7]

Change color to yellow.

Rnd 3–Rnd 6: 7sc [7]

Fasten off and leave a long tail for sewing. Sew the side of one arm between rnds 8 and 9 of the body, and sew the other side of the arm between rnds 6 and 7, so the arm is tilted at a slight angle. Sew down the rest of the arm. Make sure that the arm is in line with one of the eyes. Repeat this for the other arm.

HORNS X2

In brown

Rnd 1: Ch 3 [3]

Rnd 2: Skip first stitch, 2sc [2]

Fasten off and leave a long tail for sewing. Sew the horns between rnds 7 and 8 of the head, directly in line with each eye. The horns should be roughly 2 or 3 stitches apart.

EARS X2

In yellow

Rnd 1: Ch 5 [5]

Rnd 2: Skip first stitch, 1slst, 1sc, 2hdc [4]

Fasten off and leave a long tail for sewing. Sew the ears between rnds 7 and 8, making sure each ear is directly next to the outside of each horn.

SPOTS X4 (OR NUMBER OF YOUR CHOICE)

In brown

Rnd 1: 5sc into mc [5]

Fasten off and leave a long tail for sewing. Sew the spots randomly around the body into whatever positions you desire.

TAIL

In yellow

Rnd 1: Ch 4 [4]

Fasten off and leave a long tail for sewing.

TASSEL

Cut 3 pieces of medium-length brown yarn.

Thread one of the pieces of brown yarn through an embroidery needle. Push the needle through the starting knot at the very tip of the chain (the ch 4). Pull the brown yarn through, so it is going through the starting knot of the chain. Repeat this once more, with the second piece of brown yarn.

With the final piece of brown yarn, tie a knot around the pieces that have been threaded through the chain, to create a tassel. Trim the tassel to your desired length.

Finally, sew the tail directly between the back of the legs, between rnds 3 and 4 of the body.

PANDA

Last but not least, we have a lovely, tubby little Panda to make and adore. Isn't she sweet? This pattern results in a slightly larger project that may take quite a bit longer to make—but don't let this hold you back from crocheting an awesome creation!

MAIN BODY
Starting with the top of the head
In white

Rnd 1: 6sc into mc [6]

Rnd 2: 6inc [12]

Rnd 3: (1sc, inc) x6 [18]

Rnd 4: (2sc, inc) x6 [24]

Rnd 5: (3sc, inc) x6 [30]

Rnd 6–Rnd 10: 30sc [30]

Rnd 11: (3sc, dec) x6 [24]

Rnd 12: (2sc, dec) x6 [18]

Change color to black (see page 43 for instructions).

Stuff.

Rnd 13: In FLO, (2sc, inc) x6 [24]

Rnd 14–Rnd 15: 24sc [24]

Change color to white.

Rnd 16–Rnd 17: 24sc [24]

Rnd 18: (2sc, dec) x6 [18]

Change color to black.

Stuff.

Rnd 19: (1sc, dec) x6 [12]

Rnd 20: 6dec [6]

Fasten off and seal hole (see page 35 for instructions).

LEGS X2
In black

Rnd 1: 6sc into mc [6]

Rnd 2: 6inc [12]

Rnd 3–Rnd 4: 12sc [12]

Rnd 5: (2sc, dec) x3 [9]

Fasten off and leave a long tail for sewing. Stuff the foot lightly. Sew each foot at the base of the panda, each one directly underneath an eye. The bottom of a foot should be sewn between rnds 18 and 19 of the body. Sew the top of the foot between rnds 15 and 16 of the body. Sew down the rest of the foot. Repeat this for the other foot. Make sure that the legs are roughly 4 or 5 stitches apart.

(continued)

ARMS X2
In black

Rnd 1: 6sc into mc [6]

Rnd 2-Rnd 5: 6sc [6]

Fasten off and leave a long tail for sewing. Sew the top of the arms above each foot (roughly between rnds 12 and 13 of the body), and sew the bottom of the arms roughly between rnds 15 and 16. Sew each arm into place so it appears to be resting on the belly.

EARS X2
In black

Rnd 1: 6sc into mc [6]

Rnd 2: (1sc, inc) x6 [9]

Rnd 3: 9sc [9]

Fasten off and leave a long tail for sewing. Place each ear on a different side of the head, apart from each other. Sew the side of one of the ears between rnds 3 and 4 of the body, and sew the other side between rnds 6 and 7. Sew down the rest of the ear. Make sure that it is in line with the arms and legs. Repeat for the other ear.

EYE PATCHES X2
In black

Rnd 1: Ch 6 [6]

Rnd 2: Skip first stitch, 5sc, working on the other side of the ch (see page 38 for instructions), 5sc [10]

Fasten off and leave a long tail for sewing. Add the eyes to the top of each oval. Sew the ovals to the face at a slight angle (the tops of the ovals should be facing inward). The top of one of the ovals should be placed roughly between rnds 5 and 6 of the body, and the bottom should be placed between rnds 9 and 10. The top of the eye patches should be roughly 2 stitches apart, and the bottom of the eye patches should be roughly 5 or 6 stitches apart.

Using pink yarn, embroider a nose between the two eye patches (see page 31 for instructions).

TAIL
In black

Rnd 1: 6sc into mc [6]

Rnd 2-Rnd 3: 6sc [6]

Fasten off and leave a long tail for sewing. Sew the bottom of the tail between rnds 17 and 18 of the body and the top of the tail between rnds 15 and 16. Sew down the rest of the tail. Make sure that it is directly between the back of the two legs.

Doll FRIENDS

Finally, you've reached the most advanced section of the book: the dolls! All you need is time and patience, and soon you will be making dolls super-easily and relatively quickly!

The best bit? Once you learn how to make the Basic Doll (page 189), you can explore a range of accessories for it. You can really personalize them by experimenting with different colors and designs. There are so many hairstyle choices, too. Give them really long hair or really short hair, unravel the strands of the yarn to create different textures, or even add strands in different colors! When it comes to experimenting with different designs and ideas to achieve that perfect look, this section is completely up to you!

BASIC DOLL

Let's start with the Basic Doll: the starting point of the hundreds of different dolls that you may create! You will practice shaping and Joining Legs (page 41) for this project. If you have been following the order of this book, you should be able to make this beautiful doll relatively easily!

LEGS X2
Starting with the feet
In skin color

Rnd 1: 8sc into mc [8]

Rnd 2: 8sc [8]

Rnd 3: 2sc, 2dec, 2sc [6]

Rnd 4: 6sc [6]

Add a little bit of stuffing to the foot, to give it some shape.

Rnd 5–Rnd 7: 6sc [6]

Change color to underwear color (see page 43 for instructions).

Rnd 8: 6sc [6]

Fasten off the first leg. Keep the second leg attached.

BODY
Carrying on from the legs

Carrying on from the second leg, we will now be joining the two legs (see page 41 for instructions).

Rnd 9: Ch 2, sc into the side of the first leg (the foot should be facing forward and in line with the foot of the other leg), 5sc in the rest of the first leg, 2sc into the back of the ch, 6sc into the second leg [16]

Rnd 10: 2sc along the front of the ch, 14sc [16]

Rnd 11: 14sc, change color to skin tone (the color change should be on the hip of the doll, so you might have to modify the pattern slightly to suit your doll), 2sc [16]

Rnd 12: 5sc, dec (the dec should be on the hip of the doll, so you may need to change its placement), 6sc, dec (dec should be on the hip of the doll again), 1sc [14]

Rnd 13–Rnd 15: 14sc [14]

Stuff the body.

Rnd 16: (5sc, dec) x2 [12]

Rnd 17: 6dec [6]

(continued)

BASIC DOLL (CONTINUED)

HEAD

Carrying on from the body

Rnd 18: 6inc [12]

Rnd 19: (1sc, inc) x6 [18]

Rnd 20: (2sc, inc) x6 [24]

Rnd 21–Rnd 25: 24sc [24]

Place eyes between rnds 22 and 23, about 4 stitches apart.

Rnd 26: (2sc, dec) x6 [18]

Stuff head.

Rnd 27: (1sc, dec) x6 [12]

Continue to stuff.

Rnd 28: 6dec [6]

Fasten off and seal the hole (see page 35 for instructions).

ARMS X2

In skin color

Rnd 1: 5sc into mc [5]

Rnd 2–Rnd 7: 5sc [5]

Fasten off and leave a long tail for sewing.

Sew arms between rnds 15 and 16 on each side of the doll. (You may need to change the positioning to suit your doll accordingly.)

HAIR

For instructions, see How to Sew on Hair (page 33).

BEACH DOLL

This charming Beach Doll has a stripy swimming costume. Not only does she have the same shape as the basic doll, but she is also instantly dressed and ready for the beach! She would make perfect friends with the Mermaid (page 75) and other seaside animals.

Note: You will be making the basic doll in this pattern, BUT will be color changing for the bathing suit. Follow this pattern carefully so you do not lose your place!

LEGS X2

In skin color

Rnd 1: 8sc into mc [8]

Rnd 2: 8sc [8]

Rnd 3: 2sc, 2dec, 2sc [6]

Rnd 4: 6sc [6]

Add a little bit of stuffing to the foot, to give it some shape.

Rnd 5–Rnd 7: 6sc [6]

Change color to stripe color A (see page 43 for instructions).

Rnd 8: 6sc [6]

Fasten off the first leg. Keep the second leg attached.

BODY

Carrying on from the legs

Carrying on from the second leg, we will now be joining the two legs (see page 41 for instructions).

Rnd 9: Ch 2, sc into the side of the first leg (the foot should be facing forward and in line with the foot of the other leg), 5sc in the rest of the first leg, 2sc into the back of the ch, 6sc into the second leg [16]

Rnd 10: 2sc along the front of the ch, 2sc, change color to stripe color B (the color change should be on the hip of the doll; you may need to change this to suit your doll), 12sc [16]

Rnd 11: 16sc [16]

Rnd 12: 5sc, dec (the dec should be on the hip of the doll; you may need to change the placement to suit your doll), 6sc, change color to stripe color A (the color change should be close to the hip of the doll, so you can do a decrease on the hip of the doll in the new color), dec, 1sc [14]

Rnd 13–Rnd 14: 14sc [14]

(continued)

Change color to stripe color B (the color change should be on the hip; you may need to edit this to fit your doll).

Rnd 15: 14sc [14]

Stuff body.

Rnd 16: (5sc, dec) x2 [12]

Change color to skin tone.

Rnd 17: 6dec [6]

HEAD
Carrying on from the body

Rnd 18: 6inc [12]

Rnd 19: (1sc, inc) x6 [18]

Rnd 20: (2sc, inc) x6 [24]

Rnd 21–Rnd 25: 24sc [24]

Place eyes between rnds 22 and 23, about 4 stitches apart.

Rnd 26: (2sc, dec) x6 [18]

Stuff head.

Rnd 27: (1sc, dec) x6 [12]

Continue to stuff.

Rnd 28: 6dec [6]

Fasten off and seal the hole (see page 35 for instructions).

ARMS X2
In skin color

Rnd 1: 5sc into mc [5]

Rnd 2–Rnd 7: 5sc [5]

Fasten off and leave a long tail for sewing.

Sew arms between rnds 15 and 16, on each side of the doll (you may need to change the positioning to suit your doll accordingly).

HAIR

For instructions, see How to Sew on Hair (page 33).

DRESSES AND HEADBANDS

We will be making three different dresses that you can use for your dolls: the Blossom Dress, the Spring Dress (page 199), and the Festive Dress (page 200). The dresses have a variety of different designs, which will allow you to practice making different shapes using different techniques and stitches. Once you are comfortable making these dresses, you may even want to have a go at creating your own dress design!

We also have some headbands, which are such an adorable touch to add to your dolls. Headbands make everything so much cuter, especially if your doll looks as if she might be having a bad hair day!

BLOSSOM DRESS AND HEADBAND

DRESS

In color A

Rnd 1: Ch 21 [21]

Rnd 2: Skip first stitch, 3sc, ch 3 and skip 4 stitches, 6sc, ch 3 and skip 4 stitches, 3sc [18]

Rnd 3: Ch 1 and turn, 3sc, 3sc into the loop made last rnd, 6sc, 3sc into the loop made last rnd, 3sc [18]

Rnd 4: Ch 1 and turn, 18sc [18]

Rnd 5: Change color to B, ch 2 and turn, (1dc, dc inc) x9 [27]

Rnd 6: Ch 2 and turn, 27dc [27]

Here, you may need to add an extra rnd if the dress is not to the length you desire.

(continued)

Rnd 7: Change color to C, ch 1 and turn, 27sc [27]

Fasten off and leave a medium-length tail. Weave in the ends on the inside of the dress, and trim any excess yarn.

DRESS BELT
In color C

Rnd 1: Ch 40 [40]

Fasten off and leave a medium-length tail. Tie the belt around the waist of the doll, and then trim any excess yarn.

DRESS FLOWER
In pink (or any desired color)

Rnd 1: In mc, (ch 2, dc, slst) x5 [20]

Sew the flower onto the dress wherever you'd like it to be. Use a new color to sew a line, coming from the middle of the flower to the tip of each petal, to give the flower some extra detail. Use the flower color and new color to sew little stitches around the skirt, to give the dress extra detail.

HEADBAND
Same color used for the flower

Rnd 1: Ch 50 [50]

Rnd 2: Skip first stitch, 49slst [49]

Fasten off and leave a medium-length tail. Tie the headband around the head, and then trim any excess yarn.

SPRING DRESS AND BUNNY EARS

DRESS
In light blue

Rnd 1: Ch 21 [21]

Rnd 2: Skip first stitch, 3sc, ch 3 and skip 4 stitches, 6sc, ch 3 and skip 4 stitches, 3sc [18]

Rnd 3: Ch 1 and turn, 3sc, 3sc into the loop made last rnd, 6sc, 3sc into the loop made last rnd, 3sc [18]

Rnd 4: Ch 1 and turn, 18sc [18]

Rnd 5: Ch 2 and turn, (5dc, dc inc) x3 [21]

Rnd 6: Ch 2 and turn, 21dc [21]

Crochet tensions may vary, which result in slightly different project sizes, so you may need to add an extra rnd to the dress, depending on the height of your doll.

Rnd 7: (ch 3, 2slst) x10, ch 3, slst [21]

Fasten off and weave in the ends. Tie a piece of string around the waist of the doll and tie a bow. (This is the belt for the doll.)

HEADBAND
In white

Rnd 1: Ch 29 [29]

Rnd 2: Skip first stitch, 28sc [28]

Fasten off and leave a long tail. Sew together each end of the headband, to form a ring. Weave in any loose ends.

EARS
In white

Rnd 1: Ch 8 [8]

Rnd 2: Skip first stitch, slst, 6hdc, ch 1, working on the other side of the ch (see page 38 for instructions), 6hdc, slst [14]

Fasten off and leave a long tail. Weave in the ends, so the long piece of string is at the base of the ears. Put the headband into place on the doll. Sew the ears onto the headband, making sure that the ears line up with the eyes of the doll. The ears should be roughly 3 stitches apart. Make sure that you don't accidentally sew the ears to the head of the doll instead of just to the headband.

FESTIVE DRESS WITH BELT

DRESS
In red

Rnd 1: Ch 21 [21]

Rnd 2: Skip first stitch, 3sc, ch 3 and skip 4 stitches, 6sc, ch 3 and skip 4 stitches, 3sc [18]

Rnd 3: Ch 1 and turn, 3sc, 3sc into the loop made last rnd, 6sc, 3sc into the loop made last rnd, 3sc [18]

Rnd 4: Ch 1 and turn, 18sc [18]

Rnd 5: Ch 2 and turn, (1dc, dc inc) x9 [27]

Rnd 6: Ch 2 and turn, 27dc [27]

You may have to add an extra rnd if the dress is still shorter than you'd like it to be.

Rnd 7: Change color to white (see page 43 for instructions), ch 2 and turn, (1hdc inc, 1sc) x13, 1hdc inc [41]

Fasten off and leave a medium-length tail. Weave in the ends on the inside of the dress, and trim any excess yarn.

TRIM AT THE TOP OF THE DRESS
In white

Insert your hook through the last stitch of the very top row of stitches made in the first and second rnds of the dress, on your right-hand side. Create a slst into this stitch. Then create an inc back into the same stitch as the slst. Move to the next stitch on your left, and create a slst. Repeat the pattern (inc, slst) 9 times, until you reach the very edge of the dress.

Fasten off and weave in the loose ends.

DRESS BELT
In black

Rnd 1: Ch 40 [40]

Fasten off and leave a medium-length tail. Tie the belt around the waist of the doll, and then trim any excess yarn.

Using yellow yarn, embroider a buckle around the belt in the very center of the dress. Do this by sewing an upward running stitch to form one side of the buckle. Then create a horizontal running stitch that goes along the top of the belt. Repeat the same steps—except this time, the upward running stitch will be going downward, to create the rectangular shape. Make sure that each edge of the buckle is touching.

SUN HAT

This sun hat is just too adorable to skip! It goes perfectly as a hat for your beach doll, and it works really well with your other dolls too—especially on sunny days!

MAIN PIECE
Starting at the top
In straw color (or any other color!)

Rnd 1: 6sc into mc [6]

Rnd 2: 6inc [12]

Rnd 3: (1sc, inc) x6 [18]

Rnd 4: (2sc, inc) x6 [24]

Rnd 5: (3sc, inc) x6 [30]

Rnd 6–Rnd 8: 30sc [30]

Rnd 9: In FLO (2sc, inc, 2sc) x6 [36]

Rnd 10: (5dc, dc inc) x6 [42]

Fasten off and weave in the ends.

RIBBON FOR THE HAT
In desired color

Rnd 1: Ch 60 [60]

Fasten off and leave a medium-length tail. Wrap the ribbon around the hat into a position you like. Using a long piece of yarn of that same color, sew the ribbon to the hat, using small stitches. This is to keep the ribbon in place and ensure that it won't come off.

FLAMINGO AND DUCK FLOATIE

We have two super-cute swim rings for you.

First up is the adorable flamingo swim ring, which is a firm favorite that's perfect for some seaside fun!

Next up is the duck swim ring, which is a variation of the flamingo swim ring. These are both great fun to make—especially if you have some BFF dolls going for a swim!

For each pattern, you'll start by making the same donut ring, and then you'll create the unique head based on your desired variation.

DONUT FOR BOTH VARIATIONS

In pink or yellow, depending on the animal that you have chosen for the floatie

Rnd 1: Ch 27 [27]

Rnd 2: Skip first stitch, 26sc [26]

Rnd 3–Rnd 8: Ch 1 and turn, 26sc [26]

Fasten off and leave a long tail for sewing. Fold the crochet in half horizontally, so you have a long sausage-like shape. (If it doesn't look very long, you probably folded it the wrong way!) Sew the two sides together, stuffing the ring as you move along. Then sew each end together to form the donut shape.

FLAMINGO HEAD
Starting at the top of the head
In pink

Rnd 1: 6sc into mc [6]

Rnd 2: 6inc [12]

Rnd 3: (1sc, inc) x6 [18]

Rnd 4–Rnd 7: 18sc [18]

Place eyes between rnds 4 and 5, roughly 5 stitches apart.

Rnd 8: 9dec [9]

Rnd 9–Rnd 14: 9sc [9]

Stuff the head.

(continued)

Fasten off and leave a long tail for sewing. Sew along the bottom of the head, where the opening is, to make sure the stuffing doesn't fall out. Sew the base of the head to the donut. (If you place the donut in front of you, you want the head to be sewn to the lowest point of the donut that can be seen—you don't want to sew it too high up, or too low!) Once you have secured the base of the head, sew the rest of the neck onto the donut, so it doesn't flop forward or move around.

FLAMINGO BEAK
In black

Rnd 1: 4sc into mc [4]

Rnd 2: 4sc [4]

Change color to white (see page 43 for instructions).

Rnd 3: (1sc, inc) x2 [6]

Fasten off and leave a long tail for sewing. Sew the top of the beak between rnds 4 and 5 of the head. Sew the bottom of the beak roughly between rnds 6 and 7. Sew down the rest of the beak, to make sure it is properly secured.

DUCK HEAD
Starting at the top of the head
In yellow

Rnd 1: 6sc into mc [6]

Rnd 2: 6inc [12]

Rnd 3: (1sc, inc) x6 [18]

Rnd 4-Rnd 7: 18sc [18]

Place eyes between rnds 4 and 5, roughly 5 stitches apart.

Rnd 8: 9dec [9]

Rnd 9-Rnd 10: 9sc [9]

Stuff the head.

Fasten off and leave a long tail for sewing. Sew along the bottom of the head, where the opening is, to make sure the stuffing doesn't fall out. Sew the base of the head to the donut. (If you place the donut in front of you, you want the head to be sewn to the lowest point of the donut that can be seen—you don't want to sew it too high up, or too low!) Once you have secured the base of the head, sew the rest of the neck onto the donut, so it doesn't flop forward or move around.

DUCK BEAK
In orange

Rnd 1: Ch 4 [4]

Rnd 2: Skip first stitch, 1slst, 1sc, 1slst [3]

Fasten off and leave a long tail for sewing. Sew the beak between rnds 4 and 5 of the head, making sure that it is directly between the eyes.

BEAR BAG

Time to accessorize by styling your doll with the most adorable Bear Bag ever! Although this bag may look super-quick and easy, it is (relatively) complicated and does require some patience. However, we think it's totally worth it!

BAG FACE X2

In brown

Rnd 1: 6sc into mc [6]

Rnd 2: 6inc [12]

Fasten off the first bag face.

Keep the second bag face still attached. Align the two bag faces together, so the stitches of each face are matched together.

Rnd 3: Crochet together the two sides of the head (see page 36 for instructions), 8sc around (make sure that the top is left open, so you can put things in the bag!) [8]

Now we are going to create the bag strap.

Rnd 4: Ch 22, create a slst into the first stitch made in rnd 3 (so a loop is created for the bag strap)

MUZZLE

In beige

Rnd 1: 6sc into mc [6]

Fasten off and leave a long tail for sewing. Sew the muzzle in the middle of one of the sides of the bag. The bottom of the muzzle should be between rnds 2 and 3 of the bag face, and the top of the muzzle should be between rnds 1 and 2. Sew down the rest of the muzzle. Make sure that you don't accidentally sew the bag faces together—otherwise you won't be able to put anything inside the bag!

Using black yarn, embroider a small nose at the top of the muzzle with 1 or 2 running stitches (see page 31 for instructions).

If you would like to add safety eyes, place them directly next to each side of the muzzle. If you would like to have more space in the bag, embroider two eyes in that position instead.

EARS X2

In brown

Rnd 1: 3sc into mc [3]

Fasten off and leave a long tail for sewing. Sew one ear on each side of the opening of the bag. They should be 4 or 5 stitches apart. Make sure that they are sewn onto the bag face that has the muzzle and eyes.

BACKPACK

Make your doll this super-cool Backpack for when she goes on adventures! To make this adventurous outfit complete, you could even add the Sun Hat (page 203) in beige as an amazing explorer's hat!

BAG
Starting at the bottom of the bag
In pink/main color

Rnd 1: 6sc into mc [6]

Rnd 2: 6inc [12]

Rnd 3: (1sc, inc) x6 [18]

Rnd 4–Rnd 9: 18sc [18]

Fasten off and weave in the ends.

STRAPS X2
In blue/contrasting color

Rnd 1: Ch 12 [12]

Sew one end of a strap between rnds 8 and 9 of the bag and the other end of that strap between rnds 2 and 3 of the bag. Make sure that the strap is firmly in place, by knotting the tail ends to the inside of the bag. Repeat for the other bag strap. The bag straps should be roughly 5 stitches apart.

Using a long piece of blue yarn, weave it through the very top stitches of the bag (the stitches of rnd 9), until you reach halfway (the middle of the front of the bag—not the 5 stitches between the backpack straps). Then weave the other end of the yarn in the other direction until it meets the center, next to the other piece of yarn. Make sure that both long ends are hanging down the front of the bag (not in the inside). Pull the two pieces of yarn to tighten the top of the bag and close it. Tie a bow to keep it closed.

MINI TEDDY BEAR

Let's not forget that your doll will need a friend to keep her company! This Mini Teddy Bear is the perfect solution for this—especially since he can fit in her Backpack (page 211) and head out on adventures with her.

LEGS X2

Starting at the bottom of the leg
In brown

Rnd 1: 5sc into mc [5]

Rnd 2–Rnd 3: 5sc [5]

Fasten off the first leg.

Keep the second leg still attached.

BODY

Carrying on from the legs

Carrying on from the second leg, we will now be joining the two legs together (see page 41 for instructions).

Rnd 4: Sc into the side of the first leg, 4sc, 5sc into the second leg [10]

Rnd 5: 10sc [10]

Stuff the legs.

Rnd 6: 5dec [5]

Stuff the body.

Rnd 7: In FLO, 5inc [10]

Rnd 8: (2sc, inc) x3, 1sc [13]

Rnd 9–Rnd 10: 13sc [13]

Place eyes between rnds 9 and 10, roughly 3 stitches apart. Embroider a nose directly between the eyes, using black yarn (see page 31 for instructions).

Rnd 11: 6dec, 1sc [7]

Fasten off and seal hole (see page 35 for instructions).

EARS X2

In brown

Rnd 1: 3sc into mc [3]

Fasten off and leave a long tail for sewing. Sew one side of an ear between rnd 11 and the closing ring of the body, and sew the other side between rnds 9 and 10. Sew down the rest of the ear. The ear should be 1 stitch away from the closest eye. Repeat for the other ear.

ARMS X2

In brown

Rnd 1: 5sc into mc [5]

Rnd 2–Rnd 3: 5sc [5]

Fasten off and leave a long tail for sewing. Sew the top of one of the arms between rnds 6 and 7 of the body. Make sure that it is in line with an ear. Repeat for the other arm.

HEART BFF CUSHION

Finally, who doesn't need a Heart BFF Cushion (which also makes a great keychain gift for a friend)? This adorable cushion is perfect for your doll. Its size is just right to be cuddled, and its squidgy belly gives your doll something to snuggle up to at bedtime.

VENTRICLES X2
In pink

Rnd 1: 6sc into mc [6]

Rnd 2: 6inc [12]

Rnd 3–Rnd 4: 12sc [12]

Fasten off the first ventricle—a long tail is not needed.

Keep the second ventricle attached.

MAIN BODY OF THE HEART
Carrying on from the second ventricle

Carrying on from the second ventricle, you will be joining the two ventricles together to form the main body. This is the same method as Joining Legs (see page 41 for instructions).

Rnd 5: Put your hook through a stitch of the first ventricle and make 1sc, 11sc, put your hook into the nearest stitch on the second ventricle and make 1sc, 11sc [24]

Rnd 6: 24sc [24]

Rnd 7: (6sc, dec) x3 [21]

Rnd 8: (5sc, dec) x3 [18]

Place eyes between rnds 5 and 6, roughly 4 stitches apart. Embroider a mouth between the eyes (see page 28 for instructions). Using light-pink yarn, embroider a cheek on each side of each eye by creating two running stitches over the top of each other.

Rnd 9: 18sc [18]

Begin to stuff.

Rnd 10: (4sc, dec) x3 [15]

Rnd 11: (3sc, dec) x3 [12]

Rnd 12: 6dec [6]

Fasten off and seal hole (see page 35 for instructions).

If there is a small hole between your two ventricles, use a long piece of pink yarn and sew up the hole.

Acknowledgments

First, a huge thank you to our publishing team at Page Street—for believing in this book and guiding us in the process of creating what we hope is an essential resource to all beginner crocheters and amigurumi lovers! We are also delighted they have magically turned our words and photos into a beautifully laid out book!

We would also love to take the opportunity to thank all our wonderful pattern testers. You have been an incredibly supportive crochet community, and all your detailed feedback has been invaluable in creating this book of mini amigurumi! THANK YOU!

In alphabetical order, our amazing testers are Doreen Ainsworth, Aleena, Alice Inspired Crochet, Sheila Amborn, Josie Averill, Carrie Bear, Donna Bennett, Kimberly Berka, Christina Bladin, Justine Cresswell, Sunday Daugherty, Fruzsina Debreczeny, Kahla Dunemann, Carrie Eads, Michelle Eads, Leticia Edmonds, Gina, Tammy Graham, Samantha Grieshaber, Tracey Hamilton, Wanda Harbert (KricketKrafts), Jennifer Hawker, Suong Hoang, Dianne Hoffmeyer, Liliana Hoffmeyer, Erika Shalene Hull, Kimberly Lynn, Kelsi McKelvey, Alishka Mehra, Shayron Mooney, Robin Moran, Ania Mortellaro, Wasleya Nour, Risa Novak, Tracy Park, Pam Schremp Proctor, Megan Reetz, Lisa Schreiner, Penelope Sendor, Adrienne (Kori) Taylor, Angie Wallis, Olivia Warnero, Heidi Wentz, and Jody Wright.

About the Authors

MAGGY AND PIPPA WOODLEY are the mother-and-daughter team behind the super successful craft website and YouTube channel Red Ted Art. Red Ted Art is dedicated to helping people get creative and have crafty fun—regardless of perceived ability and skills. They firmly believe that arts and crafts are all about having a go and learning new skills! This is their first book as a team and the third book under the Red Ted Art umbrella. As their readership has grown up, so have the crafts. Their latest website focus has been on the wonderful world of crochet and all the joy it brings. They hope that you enjoy using this book, and wish you happy crocheting!

Index

The **BIG BOOK** of **BEGINNER AMIGURUMI**